Global Shocks

Nicholas P. Sargen

Global Shocks

An Investment Guide for Turbulent Markets

Nicholas P. Sargen
Fort Washington Investment Advisors
Cincinnati, Ohio, USA

ISBN 978-3-319-41104-0   ISBN 978-3-319-41105-7   (eBook)
DOI 10.1007/978-3-319-41105-7

Library of Congress Control Number: 2016949788

Cover illustration: © Ufuk ZIVANA / Alamy Stock Photo and © Apostrophe / Alamy Stock Photo

Printed on acid-free paper

This Palgrave Macmillan imprint is published by Springer Nature
The registered company is Springer International Publishing AG Switzerland

Foreword

Global Shocks provides a timely analysis of key factors contributing to a series of currency crises, asset bubbles and financial crises from the 1970s through the present. The book derives valuable insights and lessons that investors can glean from these experiences.

The seminal event is the breakdown of the Bretton Woods arrangement of adjustable parities in the early 1970s. This provided financial managers with the challenge of how to protect wealth from loss because of sharp changes in the prices of currencies, which often occurred during banking crises. A large number of currencies had fallen off steep cliffs. When currencies had been attached to parities, the managers had a relatively costless "one-way option"; they could short a currency they anticipated might be devalued and would profit if this change occurred; otherwise their losses would be trivial because the increase in the price of the currency was limited by the commitment to a parity.

The proponents of floating currencies suggested that once currencies were no longer attached to parities, this one-way option would disappear—as it has done. Some of the proponents concluded that the market in currencies was "efficient" or "not inefficient," and that the hour-to-hour and day-to-day changes in the prices of currencies would follow a random walk. They were convinced that the market prices of currencies adjusted immediately to new information and that trading in currencies would not provide exceptional profit opportunities.

What ensued, however, is nothing close to what leading advocates of flexible exchange rates had envisioned. The pattern in the data is that there are long swings in the prices of currencies, with extended periods of overshooting followed by sudden shift to undershooting. The now-standard observation is that the price of a currency in the forward market is not an effective forecast of its price in the spot market on the date that the forward contract matures—forward exchange rates tend to "under-predict" the changes in the prices of the currencies in the spot market during the term to maturity of the forward contract. The inference is that the adjustment of the prices of currencies to new information is prolonged rather than immediate and that investors have left a lot of money on the table.

Why is this so? My explanation is that proponents of floating incorrectly viewed international capital flows as being inherently stabilizing. However, as Nick Sargen's book demonstrates, the experience of the past 40 years suggests exactly the opposite: *Namely, swings in international capital flows have contributed to excessive volatility not only in currencies but also in asset prices.* These swings, in turn, are influenced by policies pursued by central banks and governments, as well as by the responses of market participants to economic developments and policies.

Global Shocks highlights three major groups of participants in currency markets. The first are goods market traders—importers and exporters who "arbitrage" differences between costs and prices of similar goods in different countries. The second are carry trade investors who seek to profit from the difference between the interest rate differential and the anticipated change in the price of the currency. The third group are money traders who profit from the long swings in the prices of currencies. They piggy-back their transactions on the buy-and-hold approach of the carry trader investors. These money traders have a hit-and-run approach to their purchases of foreign currencies; they take a position, run the profit or close the loss, put the money in the bank, and repeat the process.

One result of this interaction is that the biggest beneficiaries of the move to the floating rates have been the large banks and other firms that trade currencies; yet they have also been at the epicenter of the proliferation of financial crises since the 1980s. What can long-term investors do to protect themselves in these circumstances? A key benefit of Nick Sargen's book for investment practitioners is that it illustrates common patterns of market behavior that astute investors can exploit once they understand the driving forces behind the increased incidents of crises.

Robert Z. Aliber
June 3, 2016

Preface

This book explores how shocks that buffeted the international financial system transformed investing from "buy and hold" strategies to today's world in which investors increasingly confront asset bubbles and financial market instability. While professional investors are well schooled in the tenets of modern portfolio theory, they lack a framework for dealing with stock, bond and currency markets during periods of instability when correlations go to one. Younger investors and trainees at financial institutions are even more disadvantaged, because they only know the post-crisis environment in which interest rates have been set at zero. This book, which is written from a practitioner's perspective, fills a void by providing the reader with a toolkit and guiding principles to manage money when markets are turbulent.

I conceived the idea following the bursting of the tech bubble in the mid-2000s, when I was teaching a course at the Darden School of Business that was designed to prepare MBAs for the challenge of managing money when markets are in turmoil. It consisted of case studies of currency crises and asset bubbles since the breakdown of Bretton Woods in the early 1970s, some of which are included in this book.

This topic is especially relevant today in the wake of the 2008–09 crisis, which opened peoples' eyes to the disruptive effects financial shocks can have. With four decades of experience covering international markets, I thought I was well prepared for any situation. However, I had not experienced a situation in which financial assets sold off precipitously, and there was no place to hide other than treasuries and cash. This caused me to consider what an investor should do in these circumstances and whether there was anything in the literature to guide them.

I soon realized that previous studies of asset bubbles and financial crises, while interesting and insightful, were not directed at helping people managing money in crisis situations. A possible exception is Robert Shiller's *Irrational Exuberance*, which demonstrated how many people completely lost sight of valuations when they invested in technology and media stocks. Schiller was one of the first to claim that the US housing market was a bubble; but his behavioral explanation does not tell the full story as it does not address the reason asset bubbles and financial crisis have become more prevalent recently or the challenges rational (value-oriented) investors face when bubbles last for an extended period.

From my perspective, research conducted by economists at the Bank for International Settlements (BIS) is particularly useful in identifying the factors that contribute to asset bubbles and banking crises and in developing an early warning system to detect future bubbles.[1] A forthcoming book by Emeritus Professor Robert Z. Aliber extends the BIS analysis to consider the role international capital flows have played in contributing to four waves of currency crises and banking crises since the early 1980s. Aliber's insight suggests that crises are not isolated, and it caused me to investigate whether there are common patterns of market behavior that can be observed.

My contention is that investors who understand the common elements in crises have a better chance not only of surviving them but, ultimately, of benefiting from them. One of the principal findings of this book is that the series of currency crises that were prevalent in the 1970s and 1980s followed a predictable pattern in terms of movements in interest rates and exchange rates. However, this is not the case for the asset bubbles that ensued. In the book, I examine why asset bubbles are more difficult to detect in advance and also why they may play out differently according to the policy responses that are pursued.

The book also demonstrates how the nature of crises has evolved over the past four decades. Thus, whereas currency crises in the 1970s and 1980s were centered on deficit countries with high inflation, financial problems can occur in surplus countries with low inflation if the respective financial systems confront liquidity or solvency issues. In this respect, the task investors face in identifying potential problem areas today is more challenging than in the past, as a broader spectrum of factors must be considered, including the balance sheets of both borrowers and lenders.

Another key finding is that even if investors fail to anticipate when a bubble will burst, they can still come out ahead by investing in assets that have become over-sold. To do so, however, requires that they have a plan in place and implement it once they are confident that policymakers know what to do to stabilize financial markets and can act decisively. By following this procedure, our firm emerged in better shape after the financial crisis, and my hope is that this book will also help readers to improve their skills in detecting future crises and in developing strategies to capitalize on over-sold conditions.

Note

1. BIS research on this topic is discussed in Chap. 11 on the 2008 global financial crisis.

Acknowledgments

One of the most difficult tasks I face is to recognize the numerous people who influenced my career and the subject matter in this book. However, two people stand out—Robert Z. Aliber and Henry Kaufman.

I first met Bob Aliber 40 years ago at the San Francisco Federal Reserve Bank, and he has mentored me throughout my career. His remarkable analyses and track record makes him the best spotter of asset bubbles in the world, and he inspired me to write this book.

I had the privilege of working for Henry Kaufman in the mid-1980s and being part of the research empire he built at Salomon Brothers, which was unparalleled. Henry served as a role model for how to maintain professional standards and integrity while conducting investment research, and he hired many talented researchers, including my colleagues John Lipsky and Kim Schoenholtz. Stan Kogelman is another former Salomon colleague who has offered valuable suggestions for improving the book.

I also wish to recognize my colleagues at JPMorgan, especially Rimmer de Vries, who hired me initially, and John Olds and Susan Bell for the opportunity to serve as the global markets strategist for the Private Bank. While at Morgan, I worked with an array of highly talented people including my confidant, Shom Bhattacharya, and David Kelso, who headed the training program.

Following my career on Wall Street, I become Chief Investment Officer for the Western & Southern Financial Group under the leadership of John Barrett, who built a financial institution that is rock solid. I am also grateful to Maribeth Rahe, President of the firm's affiliate, Fort Washington Investment Advisors, and to my colleagues for the outstanding job they did in navigating our investment portfolios. Brendan White deserves special commendation for reading the manuscript and offering excellent suggestions, while Kathy Louden did an excellent job preparing it.

I wish to acknowledge the Darden Business School for allowing me to teach a course on the subject, especially Alan Beckenstein, who hired me, Edward Hess, who suggested valuable changes in my original manuscript, and George Craddock III, who oversees the Mayo Center for Investment Management. I am also grateful to Jerry Pinto of the CFA Institute for his support.

Finally, this book is dedicated to my recently-departed wife, Susan, whose memory continues to inspire me.

Contents

List of Figures

List of Tables

1

Overview: A Framework for Investing During Currency Crises and Asset Bubbles

This book is intended as a field guide to show readers how to navigate their way around, and in some cases, identify the precursors of financial crises, specifically currency crises and asset bubbles. The book features ten case studies, around which we provide comprehensive analyses of the causal forces at play, the responses of policymakers and market participants, and their ultimate resolution. It is designed to aid investors, seasoned and nascent, to develop skills for managing money when markets are not functioning normally by providing: (1) a framework to understand how markets behave during crises; (2) a process for making investment decisions; and (3) some practical guidelines for the bust phase of a bubble and the eventual market recovery.

I think of the book as a manifesto, because it represents the core beliefs about investing that I have garnered throughout my career as an international economist, global markets strategist on Wall Street and as a chief investment officer for a Fortune 500 financial institution. The experiences that are covered in each chapter are ones that transformed the international financial system and from which I derived valuable lessons in managing money.

The first half of the book covers currency crises that required coordinated policies to stabilize financial markets. They span the early 1970s to early 1990s and include the collapse of Bretton Woods; the fallout from the first two oil shocks; the consequences of the Volcker/Reagan policy regime shift in the early 1980s; the problems that Group of Three (G-3) policymakers from the USA, Germany and Japan encountered in trying to engineer an orderly decline of the dollar in the mid-1980s; and the speculative attack on the eurozone concept in 1992–93.

© The Editor(s) (if applicable) and The Author(s) 2016
N.P. Sargen, *Global Shocks*, DOI 10.1007/978-3-319-41105-7_1

The second half investigates asset bubbles that first appeared in Japan in the late 1980s and which then spread to other parts of the world. They include the 1997–98 Asian financial crisis, the bursting of the tech bubble in the early 2000s, the global financial crisis of 2008–09, and a chapter that examines whether China could become the next bubble.

While the natural inclination is to view these shocks in isolation, my objective in this chapter is to illustrate linkages that connect them. A second objective is to illustrate how these experiences can be used to draw inferences about future crises and bubbles. To do so, I present a framework that my colleague, John Lipsky, and I developed at Salomon Brothers in the mid-1980s to analyze changes in exchange rates and interest rates. The framework is then adapted to consider the asset bubbles that have become prevalent in the past 25 years.

A key difference in assessing these two types of shocks is that there are systematic patterns of market movements in the currency crises that are considered, but to a lesser extent in the asset bubbles. Consequently, my conclusion is that it is inherently more difficult for policymakers, economists and investors alike to understand the way asset bubbles play out as compared with the way currency crises typically evolve.

While the framework for analyzing asset bubbles may not improve an investor's ability to forecast future bubbles in a timely manner, it is intended to serve as a guide for investors in assessing the policy response and the market response once a bubble has burst—and the ultimate outcome. In this way, investors may be able to limit the damage from bubbles and even capitalize on them.

Inflation Transforms the World of Investing

Throughout the past four plus decades there have been remarkable changes in financial markets that have altered the investing landscape. During the 1960s investing was very simple by today's standards, because inflation was well contained, financial systems were heavily regulated and international capital flows were primarily tied to trade finance. Bond yields were low and did not fluctuate very much, so investors were content to clip coupons, and those who invested in stocks believed in holding on to them for the long run. For example, the average holding period for stocks in the post-war era through the mid-1960s was 5 years compared with 1–1.5 years in the past decade.[1]

Also, because currencies fluctuated in narrow bands around their exchange rate pegs versus the dollar under the Bretton Woods arrangement, currency risk was not pervasive.

This environment of market calm was completely overturned in the early 1970s, as international capital mobility increased and inflationary pressures gained traction, which led to the demise of the Bretton Woods system of fixed exchange rates. Throughout the remainder of the decade financial markets were dominated by a series of currency crises involving the US dollar and other perennially weak currencies such as the British pound, French franc and Italian lira. The common element was the respective inflation rates in these countries, which were considerably higher than in Germany and Switzerland and, following the first oil shock, Japan as well.

The standard toolkit for analyzing currencies at the time was fairly basic. It consisted of understanding how to interpret balance of payments statistics and how to apply the concepts of purchasing power parity (PPP) and interest rate parity (IRPT). According to PPP, exchange rate movements that exactly match inflation rate differentials between two countries should leave their international price competitiveness unaffected. IRPT is an arbitrage condition, in which interest rate differentials mirror the difference in forward and spot exchange rates between two currencies.

Assuming these conditions apply, an investor should be indifferent to holding a low-yielding currency such as the DM or Swiss franc versus a higher-yielding currency such as the US dollar or British pound, provided currency changes matched the respective differentials in inflation rates. In fact, there were large deviations from PPP throughout the 1970s. The best strategy for investors was to be long DM and Swiss francs, because these currencies appreciated more than could be explained by inflation rate or interest rate differentials. One reason is that the Federal Reserve, Bank of England and other central banks that faced rampant inflation were slow to respond, and they were continually "behind the curve." Therefore, it made sense for investors to be long currencies that were considered to be perennially strong and to short higher yielding, or "weak," currencies.

For bond investors, this strategy had the added appeal that bonds denominated in DM or Swiss francs held their value better than those denominated in dollars and sterling: While their nominal yields were below those of the USA and Britain, they did not sell off as much in an environment of rising interest rates, and thereby offered better preservation of capital.

Disinflation Alters the Equation

Just when it seemed investors had found a reliable strategy to outperform markets, policymakers in the USA and other high-inflation countries altered their behavior, realizing they needed to get ahead of expectations to convince market participants of their resolve to fight inflation. This transformation began with Margaret Thatcher's election in 1979, and it spread to the USA with Paul Volcker's appointment as Fed chairman and Ronald Reagan's election as president. The mix of tight monetary policy with expansionary fiscal policy resulted in USA and UK interest rates rising well above inflation and inflation expectations.

These developments turned conventional currency analysis on its head in the first half of the 1980s. Thus, even though the USA and UK ran large current account deficits, the dollar and sterling appreciated steadily, as high real interest rates and the commitment to support these currencies induced massive international capital flows into the USA and Britain. By the mid-1980s, however, the Reagan administration became concerned when US businesses encountered difficulty competing internationally and the economy softened. The challenge for US policymakers was to engineer a large decline in the dollar without inducing a loss of investor confidence, and they conscripted the support of Germany and Japan and other Group of Seven (G-7) policymakers in drafting the Plaza Accord.

Around that time, John Lipsky and I observed there had been a systematic pattern of changes driving the interest rate parity relationship since the breakdown of Bretton Woods. We illustrated these changes using the quadrant diagram shown in Fig. 1.1.

During the 1970s, for example, the dollar mainly operated in the northwest quadrant, which we labeled the "crisis zone," because persistent dollar weakness caused investors to demand a higher-risk premium to hold dollar assets. The monetary policy regime shift under Paul Volcker was critical to induce capital inflows to strengthen the dollar, which is depicted as a shift into the northeast quadrant. Over time, as investors became confident of the Fed's commitment, the dollar continued to strengthen even as interest rate differentials narrowed, which is depicted as a portfolio shift into the southeast quadrant. Finally, the cycle was completed when policymakers engineered an orderly decline in the dollar via coordinated monetary policy easing, which is depicted in the southwest quadrant.

The power of the quadrant diagram was that it showed a predictable clockwise rotation in the relation between changes in interest rate differentials and

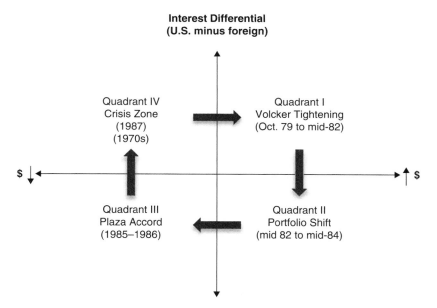

Fig. 1.1 Exchange rate changes and interest rate differentials, 1970s–1980s

movements in the dollar that held for more than a decade. In making recommendations about positioning international bond and currency portfolios, therefore, we would begin by asking which quadrant the markets were operating in at the time and where they were likely to shift next. This enabled us to make recommendations about whether to overweight or underweight international bonds versus US bonds, and whether or not to hedge the foreign currency exposure. This insight also enabled us to anticipate the need for US monetary policy to be tightened in order to stabilize the dollar in early 1987, as well as the subsequent breakdown of the Louvre Accord in the September–October period.[2]

This framework also proved useful in understanding the market forces at play in Europe in the early 1990s, when the Maastricht Treaty established criteria for a country to become a member of the euro. They included bringing the respective inflation rate in line with other members and maintaining the respective currency within the bands of the exchange rate mechanism (ERM). Investors initially embraced the eurozone concept, believing that countries on the periphery would succeed in bringing their inflation rates in line with Germany's. The so-called "convergence trade" became popular with portfolio managers, who would buy bonds in the periphery and hedge their currency exposure by selling low-yielding currencies.

The risk, however, was that this strategy became a "crowded trade," with the vast majority of international bond funds deploying it. Any event that caused investors to shift their perceptions, therefore, could result in a dramatic reversal in market forces. This occurred after Denmark rejected the Maastricht Treaty, when a group of prominent hedge fund managers, including George Soros, bet that the high-yielding bonds and currencies would sell off.

The European experience in the early 1990s differed from that of the US dollar in the prior decades in one important respect—namely, there was no clockwise rotation around the quadrant diagram. Instead, currencies in the ERM fluctuated between being in "risk on" mode (southeast quadrant) and "risk off" mode (the crisis zone), and investors had to decide which strategy was the correct one to pursue. (Note: This same type of behavior reappeared during the 2010–12 crisis in the eurozone.)

One question I have pondered is why the clockwise rotation around the quadrant diagram became less prevalent in the past two decades. My conclusion is that as central banks increasingly targeted an inflation rate of 2 %, they became more proficient in meeting their targets over time. Consequently, inflation rate differentials in the 1990s were considerably smaller than in the 1970s and 1980s (Fig. 1.2). This, in turn, meant that inflation rate differentials were not as powerful a driver of exchange rate changes as they had been previously.

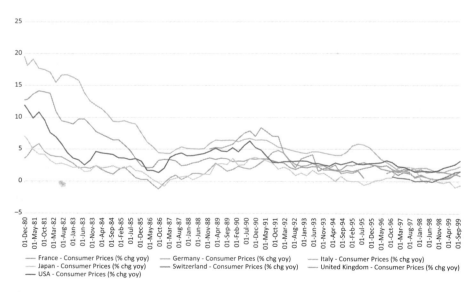

Fig. 1.2   Convergence of inflation rates, 1980 to 1999 (in %) (Source: IMF)

Emergence of Asset Bubbles

Just as central banks were winning the battle over inflation, policymakers began to encounter a new set of problems in the form of asset bubbles. This phenomenon first appeared in Japan in the late 1980s, then reappeared in Southeast Asia in the mid-1990s, before spreading to the USA and Europe during the tech bubble of the late 1990s and the housing bubble of 2003–2007. These experiences pose the following questions: (1) Why have asset bubbles become more prevalent in the past two decades? (2) Why are they especially challenging for policymakers and investors today?

With respect to the first issue, in the literature there are several approaches to asset bubbles to explain this. One is behavioral in nature, and views asset bubbles as being caused by irrational exuberance. This view is commonly associated with Robert Shiller of Yale University, who won a Nobel Prize for his work on asset bubbles in which he forecast the bubble in technology stocks in the late 1990s and that in home prices in the mid-2000s.[3] The methodology he used involved looking at deviations from long-term price trends—and the deviations in both cases were unusually large. Shiller's explanation for bubbles is rooted in human behavior and psychology.

A second approach links asset bubbles with rapid build-up in debt and easy conditions in credit markets. This view has been associated with the Austrian school of economics, and a leading proponent is William White, former economic advisor for the Bank for International Settlements (BIS), and his successor, Claudio Borio. White and Borio have written extensively on the causes of financial instability, and they led the BIS' efforts to monitor financial market instability.[4] A related approach focuses on the international dimension of asset bubbles and the pivotal role that international capital flows have played in asset booms and busts. A leading advocate of this view is Robert Z. Aliber, emeritus professor at the University of Chicago's Booth School of Business, and co-author of Charles Kindleberger's classic book, *Manias, Panics and Crashes*.[5] (For a more detailed discussion of these approaches see the Appendix to this chapter.)

Each of these approaches provide insights into the formation of asset bubbles. What is interesting about these experiences is that they occurred during a period of economic strength and low inflation—what Fed chairman Ben Bernanke termed "The Great Moderation." As William White has argued, central bankers viewed their overriding mission as restoring low inflation, but the context for setting monetary policies changed radically beginning in the mid-1970s, as financial deregulation and liberalization coincided with increased capital market integration around the world. One result of liberalization was an increase in competitive pressures in financial services and greater access to offshore funding. In addition, liberalization occurred amid a transformation of information technology that gave rise to securitization and a broad spectrum of tradeable instruments that could be used to hedge positions or to lever them.

The framework for thinking about asset bubbles presented in Fig. 1.3 depicts the southeast quadrant as their breeding ground or starting point. It is labeled the "bliss zone," because it is the phase of the economic cycle in which conditions are favorable, interest rates are low and the respective currencies are stable to strong. In this context, investors typically are optimistic about the future and eager to take risks to boost returns, including adding to higher-yielding bonds, stocks and real estate exposures. Creditors, in turn, are ready to fund such investments, as risks appear to be manageable. Meanwhile, central banks are not compelled to restrain credit growth, because inflation is under control.

Three conditions make asset bubbles more difficult for policymakers and investors to deal with than traditional currency crises. One relates to problems of detection. For example, the circumstances leading to currency crises are well known—namely, pressures build over time as the current account positions deteriorate, foreign exchange reserves are depleted and interest rates are increased to attract capital flows. By comparison, the conditions for asset bubbles are generally favorable; often there are no signs of a crisis until the

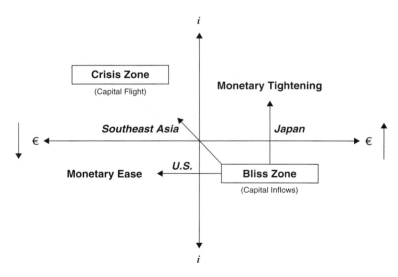

Fig. 1.3 The quadrant diagram and asset bubbles

bubble bursts. One reason is that asset bubbles often are related to balance sheets of financial institutions and their customers, and there is lack of transparency about the associated degree of financial leverage and asset-liability mismatches that contribute to the severity of problems once bubbles burst.

The common element as bubbles form is a rapid expansion in credit, which results in a build-up in debt that is considerably faster than the growth rate of the economy. In many instances the debt build-up is financed by borrowing from abroad, which creates an added element of currency risk. However, because bubbles often form over a protracted period (e.g., the second half of the 1980s and the 1990s, respectively, in the case of Japan's bubble and the US tech bubble), it is difficult to time them precisely. Yet, timing often can be the difference between success and failure in the investment world.

A second difference is that policy responses to asset bubbles are more varied than currency crises. The bursting of Japan's bubble, for example, was the result of the Bank of Japan's decision to tighten monetary policy in 1989 and to keep policy restrictive for several years. (This move is depicted in Fig. 1.2 as a shift to the northeast quadrant.) By comparison, the Asian financial crisis began with a wave of currency depreciations in Southeast Asia that catapulted the countries into the crisis zone. While monetary policies initially were tightened to stem capital flight, other measures had to be adopted when the respective banking systems were threatened.

In the case of the tech bubble and housing bubble in the USA, the policy response was the opposite—namely, the Federal Reserve lowered interest rates close to zero on both occasions and flooded the markets with liquidity, which is depicted as a shift to the southwest quadrant. This response was in keeping with the views of Fed Chairmen Alan Greenspan and Ben Bernanke that the central bank's responsibility should be to provide ample liquidity after a bubble burst, rather than to pop a bubble as the Bank of Japan did. The ability of the Fed to act in this manner, in turn, reflects two considerations: (1) the Fed is viewed by investors as a credible inflation fighter; and (2) the dollar is the world's reserve currency. Thus, despite dire warnings at the time that "twin deficits" left the USA vulnerable to capital flight, the dollar's depreciation after the tech bubble was orderly, and it strengthened after the global financial crisis of 2008–09.

Finally, a third difference is that the outcomes of asset bubbles vary considerably. The bursting of Japan's bubble, for example, was followed by two decades of stagnation and deflation. By comparison, the economies of Southeast Asia benefitted from excessive currency depreciation and experienced strong export-led growth in the following decade. In the case of the USA, the economic fallout from the subprime debacle was much more devastating than after the tech bubble burst, because the linkages to the financial sector were much greater to housing. Yet the US stock market and other risk assets experienced a powerful recovery that was fueled by a rebound in profit growth and quantitative easing by the Federal Reserve. In my view, the difference in outcomes between the USA and Japan reflects both the aggressive policy stance by the Fed, as well as the rapid adjustment by US corporations and financial institutions to the near collapse of the financial system.

Some Guideposts for Coping with Asset Bubbles

Recognizing these issues, what can investors do to protect themselves from future bubbles? My response is that there are no easy answers, as it is inherently challenging to identify bubbles in advance and to assess their impact on the economy and financial system. While it is always easy to see bubbles in hindsight, consider the challenges investors face today in determining whether China will be the next bubble to burst (this is discussed in Chap. 11).

But one thing is equally clear—investors can no longer ignore the possibility of future bubbles. My belief is that investors who are disciplined and value-oriented have the best chance of outperforming over the long run. Not only are they less likely to get caught up in a bubble mindset, but they are also more inclined to look for opportunities after a bubble has burst and others are selling securities indiscriminately. That said, the challenges that value investors face when momentum investing is in vogue should not be underestimated: As noted earlier, value investors underperformed the broad market from 1995 to 1999. The challenge then was to maintain their discipline even as they were losing assets.

The process that I follow contains four distinct stages of decision making: (1) diagnosis of the source of the problem; (2) assessment of the adequacy of the policy response; (3) assessment of the outcomes priced into markets; and (4) portfolio positioning and implementation of risk control.

Diagnosis of the Problem

In analyzing a crisis situation I begin by assessing the nature of the shock or disturbance that has unsettled financial markets. In some instances the factors contributing to a crisis are straightforward and easy to identify: for example, the impact of oil shocks or the bursting of Japan's asset bubble and the US tech bubble. In other instances, however, perceptions of a problem may change over time, as in the 1997 Asian financial crisis or the 2008 global financial crisis. Both began as relatively small problems—a currency devaluation in

Thailand and a subprime problem in the USA. However, both situations subsequently morphed to become much larger problems that threatened the entire Asia region and the global financial system. As conditions deteriorate investors face tremendous uncertainty about how they will play out, much like military leaders describe "the fog of war." Therefore, investors should not rush to judgment, but continually reassess the situation as new information unfolds. This is especially important when there is lack of transparency about balance sheet positions of financial institutions and there is a high degree of inter-dependence among economic agents.

Policy Assessment

Once a crisis unfolds, the most important thing to get right is an assessment of whether policymakers know what to do to ameliorate the situation and whether they are empowered to act boldly and decisively. The reason: Crises, by definition, imply that investors have lost confidence in policies; therefore, investors must assess what needs to be done to restore confidence. The environment for formulating new policies, moreover, often is politically charged, especially when actions being proposed have not been tried before. In the case of Japan, for example, I was reluctant to recommend the Japanese stock market to investors throughout the 1990s, because I lacked conviction about Japan's policy response to address the problem of deflation. By comparison, I drew comfort about Benjamin Bernanke's ability to stabilize the US financial system based on his knowledge of the policy failures during the Great Depression and Japan's asset bubble. The shift to quantitative easing was highly controversial at the time, as some observers believed the Fed's actions would be inflationary. However, they failed to grasp that an increase in bank reserves did not result in an accompanying increase in money supply, because bank lending remained tepid.

Market Response

One of the core tenants of sound investing is that market participants must assess what information is priced into markets and then ascertain whether or not they concur with the markets' assessment. This applies at every phase of the market cycle—during booms as well as busts. The main difference from periods in which markets are functioning normally is that what really matters is getting the big picture right. During the Japanese bubble of the late 1980s and the US tech bubble of the late 1990s, for example, the respective equity markets were priced for overall earnings growth that was several times greater than the growth of the economy. The ensuing housing bubble in the USA, in turn, resulted in home prices appreciating well past sustainable values. Once the bubble burst and the stock market sold off by 50 %, the US stock market was effectively being priced at its replacement value, which ascribes no value to current operations of the business or to value creation from future investments. While this presented investors with a tremendous buying opportunity, many stayed on the sidelines because they were afraid of losing more money.

Portfolio Positioning and Risk Control

One of the main differences in managing money during crises is that portfolio diversification may not offer adequate downside protection just when investors need it the most. The reason: Correlations among asset classes may gravitate to one. During the global financial crisis, for example, virtually all risk assets—corporate stocks and bonds, real estate, commodities and alternative investments—were hammered, and the only places to hide were "safe" assets such as cash, US treasuries and gold. Conversely, during the recovery period, risk assets far outperformed. This pattern in which markets gyrated between "risk on" and "risk off" modes was also prevalent during the eurozone crisis that began in 2010. In these circumstances, the tenets of modern portfolio theory are of little help to investors.

What strategies can investors pursue to protect themselves? Probably the most common approach is a barbell strategy, in which investors hold larger-than-normal positions in safe assets to ride out the storm, as market timing is virtually impossible in these circumstances. This approach can help dampen overall portfolio volatility, but it also runs the risk that the manager can underperform the markets and peers once markets recover. The inherent dilemma for investors is that crisis situations can present opportunities for investors to outperform materially once a sell-off has occurred that results in bargain-basement prices; however, failure to anticipate crises or to adapt to them has caused former successful money managers to have to leave the business.

My main takeaways are that investors need to spend more time thinking about risks of crises and asset bubbles, while also recognizing the inherent difficulties of detecting asset bubbles in advance. Once a bubble bursts, the key steps are to assess the problem objectively and then judge the adequacy of the policy response. If an investor lacks confidence in economic policies, it is better to stay on the sidelines than to jump back into risk assets, even if they appear cheap. Once an investor is confident that policies will improve the situation, then he or she has a better chance of performing well. In the end, my motto is to stay flexible and "live to fight another battle."

Appendix: The Role of Financial Institutions in Crises

The focus of this book is on a series of crises since the breakdown of the Bretton Woods system, which posed extraordinary challenges for investors. The main distinction that is drawn is between currency crises centered on the US dollar in the inflationary environment of the 1970s and 1980s and asset bubbles in the ensuing period of low inflation. In this appendix we highlight a third type of phenomenon that has become increasingly prevalent since the 1980s—namely, the role that banks, securities firms and so-called "shadow banks" have played as conduits for a series of financial crises.

According to Robert Aliber the past 40 years have been the most turbulent in economic history, and he identifies four waves of financial crises: (1) the LDC debt crisis in the early 1980s; (2) the Japanese real estate and stock market bubble in the late 1980s; (3) crises involving Mexico, Brazil, Argentina and emerging economies in Asia in the 1990s; and (4) a series of property bubbles in the USA, Britain, Ireland, Iceland and several other countries.[6] Aliber contends that "the likelihood that these four waves of surges in external indebtedness and in the prices of securities and currencies were independent and unrelated events is low." He also observes the close connection between banking crises and currency crises since the breakdown of Bretton Woods:

> One of the unique aspects of the past forty years is that 90 percent or more of the banking crises have been associated with a currency aspect, and every currency crisis has been associated with a banking crisis. During the 1950s and the 1960s, there were no significant banking crises and the currency crises were associated with the uncertainty about the ability and the willingness of the authorities in a country to adhere to the commitment to maintain the parities of their currencies...
>
> Since the 1980s each of the currency crises has involved a default by the borrowers in a country on the liabilities denominated in the US dollar or some other foreign currency; in some cases the liabilities were those of a government and in many other cases the liabilities were those of banks headquartered in the country that sold its IOUs in a foreign banking center to get the money so they could increase their domestic lending. The pattern in the data is that there is an increase in cross-border investment inflows, which always is associated with an increase in the trade deficit in the indebted country as the price of its currency increases, unless such increases are constrained by the intervention policies of the central bank.[7]

In terms of our quadrant diagram, the situations that Aliber is referencing are ones when markets are functioning in the "bliss zone," that is, capital inflows are associated with a strengthening currency and falling interest rates. As these situations unfold and the currency becomes overvalued, central banks typically have responded by easing monetary policies, which boost asset prices further until they reach an unsustainable level. Eventually the process reverses as capital flight results in a plummeting currency, rising bond yields and plunging asset values—i.e., markets enter the "crisis zone."

This observation raises an important issue—namely, what is it about banks and other types of financial institutions that often makes them the conduit for crises? In the wake of the 2008 global financial crisis, there has been greater appreciation of Hyman P. Minsky, an original thinker whose work had largely been ignored by the economics profession.[8] Minsky's central thesis is that finance in a capitalist system is inherently pro-cyclical and unstable, which has been called the "financial instability hypothesis." The essence of the argument is that banks and other financial institutions are willing to make loans on attractive terms during periods when economic conditions are favorable; however, they subsequently become reluctant to roll over credits when perceptions of the economy begin to deteriorate, which some have called "the Minsky moment."

Having spent a good part of my career on Wall Street, I can relate to this type of behavior. I first observed it during the oil shocks of the 1970s and early 1980s, when multinational banks saw profitable opportunities lending to less developed countries (LDCs) and rolled over credits routinely until the moment when countries such as Mexico, Brazil and Argentina (also known as MBAs) ran out of foreign exchange reserves. A critical mistake bankers made was the failure to appreciate that economic growth in these countries was being boosted temporarily by the net increase in capital flows; however, the proceeds did not earn the necessary return to cover the debt service costs when the external environment turned unfavorable. They did not foresee a situation in which banks collectively would become reluctant to roll over credits, such that the borrowers could no longer service their debts out of new loans. During the LDC debt crisis, most of the borrowing was by sovereign entities from multinational banks, who themselves were at risk of insolvency when their loans to the MBAs far exceeded their capital.

During the 1990s, multinational banks believed these countries had learned the error of their ways, as countries such as Mexico and Argentina no longer ran outsized budget deficits. While their current account imbalances remained large, they mainly reflected borrowing by private institutions including local banks, which the multinational banks regarded as less risky than loans to sovereigns. However, when Mexico's exchange rate proved to be overvalued and capital flowed out of the country following a presidential election in 1994, the same pattern of capital flight, currency depreciation and plummeting asset values occurred. Faced with yet another debacle in Latin America, multinational banks subsequently shifted their priority to countries in emerging Asia, which then encountered problems in the form of a commercial real estate bubble (this is discussed in Chap. 8).

Increased Frequency of Financial Crises

The question that these types of experiences beg is: "Why have financial crises become increasingly pervasive since the 1980s?" The most common explanation points to major changes that occurred in regulatory structures that contributed to more rapid expansion of both domestic credit and international capital flows. One is that the USA and other developed economies dismantled outdated regulatory structures (such as interest rate ceilings in the USA that were part of Reg. Q) in favor of financial deregulation that was intended to improve overall resource efficiency. This was followed by the dismantling of Glass-Steagall provisions in the late 1990s, which allowed commercial banks and investment banks to compete directly. The second is that Japan and countries in Europe liberalized foreign exchange restrictions to permit a freer flow of international capital. In the case of Japan, this move was necessitated by the massive build-up in the country's foreign exchange reserves, while in Europe the elimination of capital controls was part of the effort to create a single currency. The third development was the growth of "shadow banks"—i.e., various types of financial institutions that perform functions similar to commercial banks, but which do not have demand deposits and therefore are not subject to the same regulatory oversight. The role these institutions played during the 2008 global financial crisis is discussed in Chap. 10.

In addition to these considerations, researchers at the BIS have pointed to an added factor—namely, the role central banks have inadvertently played in facilitating rapid credit expansion. The argument that William White and Claudio Borio have made is that while central banks have been successful in keeping inflation in check, they have not paid adequate attention to the expansion of credit both by banks and non-bank financial intermediaries, which in their view has sown the seeds for financial crises. The BIS researchers, in turn, have conducted extensive research to identify the key determinants of financial cycles, which typically last 15–20 years and can span several business cycles.[9] One of the key findings is that financial crises are closely correlated with property bubbles:

While there is no consensus definition of the financial cycle, the broad concept encapsulates joint fluctuations in a wide set of financial variables including both quantities and prices. BIS research suggests that credit aggregates, as a proxy for leverage, and property prices, as a measure of available collateral, play a particularly important role in this regard. Rapid increases in credit, particularly mortgage credit, drive up property prices, which in turn increase collateral values and thus the amount of credit the private sector can obtain. *It is this mutually reinforcing interaction between financing constraints and perceptions of values and risks that has historically caused the most serious macroeconomic dislocations.*[10] (Italics added)

Classifying Shocks in This Book

Using the above framework we have classified the various shocks in this book, shown in Table 1.1, which depicts whether they entailed one or more of the following characteristics: (1) a currency crisis; (2) an asset bubble; and (3) a banking or financial crisis. The shocks that are featured in the respective chapters of the book are depicted in the rows and the three categories of crises are shown in the columns. From the table it is evident that the high inflation era of the 1970s and 1980s was dominated by a series of currency crises involving the US dollar, which required extraordinary policy actions to stabilize markets; however, the only financial crisis of note occurred during the LDC debt crisis, when the MBAs and other less developed countries ran out of foreign exchange reserves and the value of the loans extended to them were written down by banks over time.

By comparison, the shocks that have occurred since then in a low-inflation environment have all been associated with asset bubbles, and the ones that

Table 1.1 Classifying the shocks

Shock	Currency crisis/ problem	Asset bubble	Financial crisis
Bretton Woods collapse	Weak dollar		
Oil shocks (I & II)	Weak dollar		
LDC debt crisis	MBAs		Yes
Oct '87 stock crash	Weak dollar	Yes	
Attack on ERM ('92–'93)	High-yield currencies		
Japan bubble	Strong yen	Yes	Yes
Asia crisis	Yes	Yes	Yes
Tech bubble		Yes	
2008 financial crisis		Yes	Yes
China bubble		Yes	unknown

were the most severe were accompanied by banking or financial crises. The principal exception was the tech bubble, where banks and financial institutions on the whole did not have excessive exposure to tech stocks. Consequently, the Fed was able to contain the damage from the bubble and the recession was fairly mild. The fallout from the bursting of the housing bubble was considerably greater, because homes are a major source of wealth for households, and financial institutions had considerable exposure, direct or indirect, to housing that was also highly leveraged.

Finally, this classification may be helpful as we consider—in the final chapter—the possibility that China could be the next bubble to burst. My main worry is that there is a significant property bubble in China that could burst when credit conditions tighten, and which has potential to create sizeable losses for financial institutions. However, because the financial system is predominantly government controlled, there may not be a western-style banking crisis. Nonetheless, China would still face problems associated with poor resource allocation that could cause the economy to slow considerably in the future.

Notes

1. See Michael Mauboussin and Dan Callahan, Credit Suisse, "A Long Look at Short-Termism," November 18, 2014.
2. See Salomon Brothers Bond Market Research reports, "The US Dollar: Obstacles to Stabilization," October 10, 1986 and "Testing the Louvre Accord," September 3, 1987.
3. Shiller's most famous book, *Irrational Exuberance*, is discussed in Chap. 9.
4. White has written numerous articles on financial instability. His views are discussed in Chap. 11.
5. In addition to updating *Manias, Panics and Crashes*, Aliber is completing a book titled *The Source of Financial Crisis*.
6. Ibid.
7. Ibid., p. 26.
8. For a discussion of Minsky's theories, see L. Randall Wray, *Why Minsky Matters: An Introduction to the Work of a Maverick Economist*, Princeton University Press, December 2015.
9. See BIS, 84th *Annual Report*, Chapter 4, June 2014.
10. Ibid., pp. 65–66.

Part I

Investment Challenges in a High Inflation Era

2

Bretton Woods' Collapse Alters the World of Investing

One of the landmark developments influencing financial markets in the post-war era was the shift in the international monetary system from a fixed to a floating exchange rate regime in the early 1970s. The demise of the Bretton Woods (BW) system of fixed exchange rates was a milestone event that marked the end of a prolonged period of low inflation and strong economic growth in the major industrial countries. It was heralded by President Nixon's decision to suspend convertibility between the US dollar and gold at a fixed price of $35 per ounce in August 1971. The announcement occurred as I was en route from graduate school at Stanford University to my first job at the US Treasury Department, and I recall wondering "Why did he do it?" and "What does it mean?"

The answer to the first question became apparent when I arrived at the research department of the Office of the Assistant Secretary for International Affairs that was headed by Paul Volcker. Officials at the US Treasury, which oversees US exchange rate policy, were concerned that the USA had a balance of payments problem, as manifested in a steady outflow of gold and a bur-geoning trade deficit that they feared would grow over time. They hoped that closing the gold window would dampen speculation on the dollar and that an 8–10 % devaluation of the dollar would restore US price competitiveness internationally.

These hopes were dashed when pressures on the dollar resurfaced soon after, amid soaring US and global inflation. The dollar was devalued for a second time in February 1973, and attempts to reinstate new parities were abandoned in the wake of the first oil shock in the autumn. Few people at the time foresaw the decade of high inflation and economic instability that ensued. As

© The Editor(s) (if applicable) and The Author(s) 2016
N.P. Sargen, *Global Shocks*, DOI 10.1007/978-3-319-41105-7_2

two decades of strong equity performance and low interest rate volatility gave way to large gyrations in financial markets, investors abandoned "buy and hold" strategies and were forced to develop new approaches to make money and preserve wealth. Indeed, the world of investing was never the same.

Today, few people believe that a system along the lines of Bretton Woods can be replicated, given the tremendous mobility of international capital and the desire of countries to maintain independent monetary policies. Nonetheless, many observers still look back fondly at the period of economic prosperity and financial stability associated with it.

Origins of Bretton Woods

For roughly 25 years after World War II, the international monetary system was governed by a set of arrangements that western governments adopted at the Bretton Woods Conference in 1944. The overriding objectives of policy-makers at that time were: (1) to establish an exchange rate system that would foster low inflation and free trade; and (2) to ensure that the system was also sufficiently flexible to promote long-term economic growth and development.

The goals set out at the conference were largely a response to developments between the two world wars. The gold standard that prevailed before World War I succeeded in achieving the first objective—price stability—because central banks had to maintain a strict relation between their domestic money supplies and their holdings of gold. However, this requirement proved to be a double-edged sword when deflation surfaced in the 1930s: Countries that experienced an outflow of gold reserves were obligated to contract their domestic money supplies.

Ultimately, as the Great Depression worsened, many countries were forced to abandon the gold standard, and competitive depreciations ensued, as countries pursued "beggar my neighbor" policies. With the onset of World War II, there was a complete breakdown in the system of free trade and capital flows that had prevailed at the end of the nineteenth century.

The challenge for policymakers in the post-war period was to create a new international monetary system that would preserve the discipline inherent in the gold standard, while also allowing for greater flexibility as global economic conditions changed. Toward this end, the BW participants embraced a system of *fixed but adjustable par values*.

Under this arrangement, every country that became a member of the newly established International Monetary Fund (IMF) was required to establish a par value for its currency in terms of gold. If countries incurred temporary balance of payments problems—i.e., their official holdings of gold, US dollars and other reserve currencies declined—they could borrow funds on a short- or medium-term basis from the IMF. Countries were also allowed to alter their exchange rates by changing their par values if it became apparent that the external payments imbalances were persistent and there was a "fundamental disequilibrium."

While the BW system preserved some features of a gold standard, it actually operated as a US dollar-exchange standard. The par value for the dollar, for example, was set at $35 per ounce, and the provision of convertibility meant that the US government was obliged to buy and sell gold freely at this price for settling international transactions. Thus, a surplus country would accumulate external reserves and could choose to add to holdings of gold or dollars (usually in the form of US Treasury debt), while a deficit country would cover its imbalance either through sales of gold or US dollars. In practice, settlements typically occurred in dollars, because the US government was free to create new debt obligations, while the supply of gold was limited. In effect, this meant the dollar served both as a vehicle currency for financing international trade and capital flows, as well as a store of value for holding official reserves.

A Smooth Start

At the time the BW system was being formulated, the outlook for the global economy was highly uncertain. Many prominent economists, including John Maynard Keynes, believed there was a significant risk that the US economy could revert into a depression as peace ensued. Keynes' main worry was that there would be a shortage of international liquidity, and he proposed the creation of an international currency to lessen the possibility. Others, including Harry Dexter White, who headed the US Treasury representation at the 1944 conference, thought the most important post-war problem was the threat of competitive depreciations and discriminatory exchange controls.

These pessimistic views, however, proved to be far off the mark, as the US and the global economy benefitted from low inflation and a post-war recovery that lasted through the first half of the 1960s. From the early 1950s to the mid-1960s, for example, US consumer price inflation stayed at around 2 %, while real gross domestic product (GDP) growth averaged about 3½ %, reflecting an expanding labor force and strong productivity growth. Conditions abroad were also resilient, as Germany and Japan recovered from the war, assisted by the USA and its allies.

Financial assets thrived in this environment. Short-term interest rates in the USA typically were at 2–3 %, while Treasury bond yields consistently were below 4 %. The US stock market enjoyed its best performance on record, with annual returns close to 20 % in the 1950s and in double digits in the first half of the 1960s.[1]

In this environment, most countries were able to maintain their par values, and international reserves expanded in line with growth of the world economy and international trade. As a result, there were relatively few strains on the international monetary system.

Balance of Payments Pressures in the 1960s

The US balance of payments surfaced as an issue in the 1960 presidential election. During the election campaign, John Kennedy expressed concern that the USA was experiencing an outflow of gold for the first time in the post-war era. Most economists at the time viewed the outflow as a natural development, considering the strong post-war recovery in Europe and Japan, which was accompanied by an increase in the demand for international reserves.

Nonetheless, in 1963 the US government imposed a federal tax of 15 % on interest received from foreign borrowers. The interest equalization tax (IET) was designed to diminish capital outflows by making it more expensive for foreign borrowers to raise funds in the USA. Its actual effect, however, was to stimulate the development of the Eurodollar market by driving dollar-based financing activity to London.

Strains on the international monetary system intensified in the second half of the 1960s, as US economic policies turned highly expansionary. President Lyndon B. Johnson embarked on an ambitious program to improve the plight of the poor ("The Great Society") at the same time that the USA was becoming increasingly involved in the Vietnam War. During this period, the federal budget shifted into deficit, while the Federal Reserve pursued an accommodative monetary policy, supplying ample liquidity to the financial system. US interest rates rose as the economy boomed, but not enough to contain inflation, which accelerated to 4 %.

This situation created problems for European policymakers, especially those in Germany, Holland and Switzerland, where the primary objective of monetary policy was to keep inflation low, typically at 2 % or less. These countries accumulated international reserves, as their trade surpluses expanded, and their domestic money supplies expanded as exporters exchanged dollars for domestic currency. The Bundesbank, Swiss National Bank and other central banks attempted to counter this trend by draining liquidity from the financial system. However, the upward pressure on European interest rates attracted international capital flows from abroad, which made it increasingly difficult for these central banks to control their money supplies.

Tensions continued to mount as US inflation reached 5 % in 1969–70, and the USA began to run a trade deficit for the first time. European officials complained that Europe was importing inflation from the USA, because central banks were obliged to buy dollars at a fixed exchange rate, and the USA was not constrained by the balance of payments from creating more dollars.

Most of the increase in capital outflows from the USA were short term and appeared in the "other" and "errors and omissions" categories of the US balance of payments (Table 2.1). As foreign central banks accumulated unwanted dollar foreign exchange reserves, they increasingly sold their dollars for gold. By the summer of 1971, US official holdings of gold, which totaled nearly $30 billion at the end of World War II, were down to just over $10 billion, and hundreds of millions of dollars were being withdrawn each month.

Negotiating a Dollar Devaluation

Conditions reached breaking point in August, when President Nixon startled the world by announcing that the USA was closing the gold window, ending the convertibility of gold into dollars. This action, by itself, did not herald the end of the Bretton Woods system, as the USA still favored a system of fixed exchange rates. But it marked the beginning of the end of the system. At the same time, President Nixon announced a system of wage and price controls to keep inflation in check.

Table 2.1 US balance of payments (billions of dollars)

	1968	1969	1970	1971	1972	1973
Trade balance	0.6	0.6	2.6	−2.3	−6.4	0.9
Current account	0.6	0.4	2.3	−1.4	−5.8	7.1
Capital flows						
Direct investment	−4.5	−4.7	−6.1	−7.3	−6.8	−8.5
Portfolio investment	2.8	1.6	1.2	1.2	3.9	3.2
Other	2.2	6.9	−7.9	−13.2	−0.5	−4.4
Errors and omissions	0.5	−1.5	−0.2	−9.8	−1.9	−2.6
Overall balance	1.7	2.7	−10.7	−30.5	−11.0	−5.2
Note: Liabilities to foreign central banks	−0.8	−16	7.4	27.4	10.3	5.1

Source: IMF Yearbook

Over the next three months, US officials met with their counterparts in Europe and Japan to negotiate the first devaluation of the dollar. The main objective of US Treasury officials was to achieve a depreciation of the dollar that would help restore US international price competitiveness. They were particularly concerned that a burgeoning US trade deficit would grow steadily over time if the US dollar maintained its parities versus the Japanese yen and the key European currencies. The research department where I worked was assigned the task of estimating how much the dollar needed to depreciate against these currencies to restore US price competitiveness. The conclusion was that a depreciation of 8 % to 10 % should be sufficient.

At the Smithsonian meeting in December, Treasury Secretary Connelly startled his European and Japanese counterparts when he announced that the US government favored a 20 % depreciation of the dollar. This, in fact, was a bargaining ploy, as US officials believed that the Europeans and Japanese would only sanction 5 % depreciation, which would not be sufficient to improve the US trade situation.[2] In the end, a compromise was reached, whereby the dollar was devalued by about 8 %. Thus, a new par value for the dollar was set at $38 per ounce; however, the US was no longer obliged to exchange dollars for gold at this price.

The Interregnum

While these policy actions stabilized the currency markets temporarily, pressures on the dollar resurfaced before too long, when the US trade position failed to improve and Japan's trade moved increasingly into surplus. At the same time, strains developed within Europe: Countries with trade surpluses such as Germany, Holland and Switzerland experienced upward pressures on their currencies, while those with trade deficits such as the UK, France and Italy saw their currencies come under pressure.

In order to maintain the Smithsonian exchange rate parities, the Federal Reserve was obliged to tighten monetary policy while the central banks of the surplus countries were obligated to ease monetary policies. Both sides, however, were reluctant to change their monetary policies. The surplus countries intervened heavily in the foreign exchange markets to maintain the new exchange rate pegs, accumulating dollar reserves in the process. But their efforts to drain liquidity in their domestic money markets proved ineffective, because capital flowed into these countries as the central banks attempted to leave interest rates unchanged.

This situation resulted in renewed bickering between US officials and policymakers in the surplus countries, especially as they accumulated massive holdings of unwanted dollars, and inflation accelerated around the world. By 1973, holdings of dollar reserves of the Bundesbank and Bank of Japan had tripled from the levels at the start of the decade, and the reserves of all industrial countries nearly doubled (Table 2.2). The increase in global foreign exchange reserves, in turn, was accompanied by a massive surge in commodity prices. The IMF's index of commodity prices, for example, rose by about 75 % from 1971 to 1973, while the price of gold on the open market soared well above the $38 official price.

The pressures on the dollar became insurmountable, as foreign central banks grew reluctant about accumulating dollar reserves, and increasingly switched out of dollars and into gold. Foreign exchange traders smelled blood and began to sell dollars, adding to the pressures.

The situation reached breaking point in February 1973, when officials threw in the towel and closed the foreign exchange markets. Officials from the USA and other industrial countries huddled to negotiate the second devaluation of the dollar, and agreed on a new par value for the dollar of $42 per ounce of gold. This time, however, officials realized it was senseless to commit to a new set of fixed exchange rate parities, unless they could agree on the policy actions that were needed to reduce inflation and trade imbalances between the USA and the surplus countries. Thus, when the foreign exchange markets were reopened, currencies for the first time were free to fluctuate as a result of market forces. Central banks, however, were still committed to intervene in currency markets whenever they believed that exchange rate changes were excessive or "disorderly."

Table 2.2 Total reserves (billions of Special Drawing Rights)

	Industrial countries	USA	Germany	Japan
1965	58.9	15.4	7.4	2.1
1966	59.4	14.9	8.0	2.1
1967	60.2	14.8	8.2	2.0
1968	61.4	15.7	9.9	2.9
1969	60.6	17.0	7.1	3.6
1970	72.6	14.5	13.6	4.8
1971	99.2	12.2	17.2	14.8
1972	113.4	12.1	21.9	16.9
1973	111.6	12.0	27.5	10.1

Source: IMF Yearbook

A "Managed" System of Floating Exchange Rates

The shift from fixed to floating exchange rates, in short, was less the result of a decision that floating rates were desirable, as much as a realization that it was the only feasible arrangement in a context of high world inflation and increased capital mobility. Milton Friedman, a long-standing proponent of flexible exchange rates, maintained that this was a healthy development, because it allowed countries that were committed to low inflation to regain control of their money supplies. Also, to the extent that surplus countries experienced appreciation of their currencies, it would tend to reduce the size of their surpluses.

For some economists and policymakers, however, the lapse into floating exchange rates was a negative development, because it signaled the end of a system that helped foster the growth of international trade and capital flows in the post-war era. While countries were now free to pursue independent monetary policies, these skeptics believed that a floating exchange rate system was inherently unstable, because countries no longer were constrained by their balance of payments. Indeed, inflation continued to surge in the USA and most other countries following the breakdown of BW (Table 2.3).

Any hopes that the system could be re-established were dashed in autumn 1973, when OPEC responded to the outbreak of hostilities in the Middle East by announcing an embargo on oil exports. Inflation soared in the industrial world as oil prices quadrupled, and payments imbalances between oil-exporting and oil-importing countries reached magnitudes that had never been seen before. Accordingly, policymakers in the industrial countries worried less about exchange rate volatility and refocused their efforts on stabilizing the world economy.

Fixed Versus Floating Exchange Rates: A Post-Mortem

During the period surrounding the breakdown of BW there was a lively debate among economists about the consequences of abandoning fixed exchange rates in favor of flexible exchange rates. Critics of flexible exchange rates argued

Table 2.3 CPI inflation (in %)

	Industrial countries	USA	Germany	Japan
1970	5.6	5.9	1.9	7.7
1971	5.2	4.3	3.4	6.4
1972	4.7	3.3	5.2	4.9
1973	7.7	6.2	5.5	11.7
1974	13.3	11.0	7.0	23.1

Source: IMF Yearbook

that increased uncertainty and transaction costs would dampen growth of international trade and direct investment. They also maintained that a system of floating exchange rates was inherently unstable, and pointed to the experience of flexible exchange rates in the 1920s as proof of this proposition. (In an influential study of this period, Ragnar Nurkse argued that currency markets were subject to "destabilizing speculation," and flexible exchange rates would result in currency fluctuations that damaged economic growth.[3])

Milton Friedman challenged this assertion in a seminal article written in 1952, in which he maintained that the currency instability during the 1920s was caused by unstable economic policies, and not by destabilizing speculation.[4] The essence of his argument was theoretical: He contended that profit-maximizing speculators would tend to stabilize the exchange rate; otherwise they would lose money. This presumes, however, that currency-market participants are primarily value-driven rather than price- or momentum-driven, which is an empirical issue.

One of the handicaps that economists encountered was that there was little experience with flexible exchange rates in the post-war era. The only industrial country to pursue such a policy was Canada during the period from 1950 to 1962. By and large, the Canadian experiment was perceived favorably, as the Canadian dollar was relatively stable throughout this period. Based on this experience, proponents of flexible exchange rates believed that a generalized system of flexible exchange rates would operate in a similar fashion.

Today, with 40 years of experience with floating exchange rates, even the most ardent supporters would concede that currency fluctuations have been much greater than expected. Indeed, Robert Aliber has observed that beginning with the breakdown of the Bretton Woods system, "There have been more foreign exchange crises than in any previous period of comparable length."[5]

For the most part, purchasing power parity (PPP) worked reasonably well in anticipating the direction of currency movements during the 1970s, but not the magnitudes. In an influential article written in 1976, Rudiger Dornbusch provided an explanation of why exchange rates are much more volatile than inflation rates or money supplies.[6] The article provided a rationale to explain how, even without destabilizing speculation, currencies could "overshoot" their long-run equilibrium values.

While there were large deviations from PPP in the 1970s, countries with chronic high inflation rates and trade deficits (e.g., the USA, the UK and France, among others) tended to have weak currencies, while those with low inflation rates and trade surpluses (e.g., Germany, Switzerland and Japan) tended to have strong currencies. In this respect, currency changes were compatible with current account adjustment.

As discussed in subsequent chapters, this relationship broke down in the first half of the 1980s, when both the US dollar and the British pound appreciated considerably in both nominal and real terms, even though the USA and the UK had higher inflation rates than their trading partners and ran large current account deficits. Throughout this period, currency analysts who focused on inflation rates and trade balances predicted that the dollar and sterling would weaken significantly, only to see these currencies appreciate steadily. These analysts did not fully grasp the significance of monetary policy regime shifts in the USA and the UK and their effects in lowering inflation expectations and in restoring investor confidence.

While critics of flexible exchange rates were correct about currency swings being much larger than anticipated, their assumption that it would hinder growth of international trade and direct investment was not validated. One explanation that has been put forth is that many international businesses appear to have followed a strategy of "pricing to market," in which they keep stable the prices of their exports in terms of the importing country's currency. By absorbing the effect of exchange rate changes into their profit margins, companies can mitigate the effect of currency fluctuations on export volumes.

Another explanation is that countries within various regions have formed trading blocs or currency blocs to help dampen the impact of exchange rate changes. For example, the large swings in values of European currencies throughout the 1970s provided impetus for the creation of the European Monetary System (EMS) in 1979. The most important component of the EMS was the Exchange Rate Mechanism (ERM), which committed the member countries to keep their exchange rates within narrow bands. This was designed to mitigate the impact of currency fluctuations on trade flows and on domestic prices.

In the wake of all these developments, views among economists about the desirability of fixed versus floating exchange rates have changed over time. Today, most concur with the assessment that it is impossible to reinstate a regime along the lines of Bretton Woods, because of their vulnerability to speculative attacks. However, it is also accepted that no single exchange rate regime may apply for all countries.[7]

So, which economic concept that was formulated in the 1960s has stood the test of time? My answer—the concept of the impossible trinity that was formulated by Robert Mundell.[8] It states that among the following choices policymakers can choose any two: (1) fix the exchange rate; (2) conduct an independent monetary policy; and (3) allow capital to flow freely into and out of the country. Thus, if they opt to restrict capital flows, they can pursue an independent monetary policy while setting a fixed exchange rate. However, if they permit international capital to flow freely and wish to pursue independent monetary policy, they must allow the exchange rate to fluctuate.

Financial journalist Steven Solomon, in his book *The Confidence Game*, eloquently summarizes the change in the financial environment that occurred following the breakdown of Bretton Woods:

> World finance, as designed at Bretton Woods, New Hampshire, in July 1944, consisted of segregated national islands with limited exchange among them to finance trade and direct investment and some financial investing. This arrangement created a buffer among nations that permitted each government great latitude to regulate how capital coursed through its financial system into its domestic economy. Internationally, governments managed the cross-currency exchange rates in defense of a free trade regime. This prosperous postwar order has been pithily summed up as "Keynes at home, Smith abroad."[9]

The massive increase in international capital flows since the early 1970s had forever altered the equation, such that capital is now allocated primarily through private rather than official channels. Here, Solomon observes:

> Global capital mobility caused government's sovereign control over national savings and national monetary policy to slip away – or more specifically, to be pooled. George Shultz characterizes the new era as one in which the "court of the allocation of world savings" every day judges the economic policies of governments, rewarding those it favored with investment and strong currencies and punishing others by withholding capital and weak currencies.[10]

Conclusions

The collapse of the Bretton Woods system, which proved to be transformational for the global financial system, began just as I was starting my career as an international economist at the US Treasury Department. Using the framework spelled out in the previous chapter, I offer the following assessment of what happened.

Diagnosis of the Problem

Views at the time were divided between those of the US Treasury, which contended that the USA faced a balance of payments problem, and those of European and Japanese officials, who maintained that the USA had become a high-inflation country and was exporting inflation to the rest of the world. While I worked at the Treasury, I fell into the trap of being preoccupied with the need to address the US trade imbalance, even though it was miniscule by today's standards. It was not until I worked at the Federal Reserve Bank of San Francisco in the mid -1970s that I gained a better understanding of the role US monetary policy played in contributing to inflation via rapid money supply expansion.

Policy Response

The US policy response of closing the gold window and devaluing the dollar proved to be inadequate, because it did not address the problem of accelerating US inflation. Thus, while the Federal Reserve raised interest rates in the late 1960s and early 1970s, real interest rates—interest rates adjusted for inflation expectations—were low or negative. This meant the Fed was continually behind the curve when it raised interest rates.

Market Response

The market response was that the dollar became chronically weak, US bond yields surged and financial markets performed poorly—all symptoms that the USA was operating in the "crisis zone."

Portfolio Positioning

While I did not manage investment portfolios at the time, I became a dollar bear and shunned the US stock market after 1973, preferring to invest in real estate as a hedge against inflation. Like many other Americans, I learned that the best way to be protected against inflation and high-marginal tax rates was to get deeper into debt.

Notes

1. Ibbotson Associates, Stocks, Bonds, Bills and Inflation, *2003 Yearbook.*
2. Note: Information based on internal briefings at the US Treasury Department.
3. Ragnar Nurkse, *International Currency Experience*, 1942.
4. Milton Friedman, "The Case for Flexible Exchange Rates," in *Essays in Positive Economics*, 1953.
5. See *Manias, Panics and Crashes,* Chapter 13 "The Lessons of History of the Most Tumultuous Deacdes Ever," p. 278. Aliber also notes that there were more asset bubbles in the period following the collapse of Bretton Woods than in any earlier period.
6. Rudiger Dornbusch, "Expectations and Exchange Rate Dynamics," *Journal of Political Economy*, 84 (1976).

7. As part of its surveillance mandate, the IMF has produced three major analytic studies on countries' choices of exchange rate regime, which have arrived at different conclusions.
8. Robert Mundell, "Capital Mobility and Stabilization Policy Under Fixed and Flexible Exchange Rates," *Canadian Journal of Economics and Political Science*, November 1963.
9. Steven Solomon, *The Confidence Game*, Simon & Shuster, New York, 1995, p. 38.
10. Ibid., p. 39.

3

Oil Shocks Generate Massive Payments Imbalances

One of the key factors contributing to strong world economic growth and low inflation in the post-World War II era was an abundance of cheap energy. Following a period of near-price stability in the 1960s, oil prices began to rise in the early 1970s along with many other commodities. Even then, the price of oil was only about $3 per barrel, and gasoline at the pump was about $0.30 per gallon.

The world of cheap energy vanished quickly, however, following the conflict between Israel and the Arab states in autumn 1973. Members of the Organization of the Petroleum Exporting Companies (OPEC) imposed an embargo on oil exports that resulted in oil prices surging to $12 per barrel within a matter of months. The quadrupling of oil prices, in turn, unleashed a series of events that posed new challenges for industrial and developing countries.

Investors at the time also faced a host of issues they had never confronted before:

- Was the shortage of oil likely to be temporary or long term; and where were prices headed over the medium and long term?
- What impact would higher oil prices have on the global economy and inflation; and how would policymakers respond?
- How easily could the international financial system recycle funds from the surplus oil-exporting countries to the deficit oil-importing countries?

While the first two oil shocks took a considerable toll on the global economy—both resulted in rising bond yields and severe recessions—the US dollar

N.P. Sargen, *Global Shocks*, DOI 10.1007/978-3-319-41105-7_3

and stock market fared much better following the second shock. Subsequent oil shocks in the 1990s and early 2000s also were accompanied by recessions; however, they were less severe—in large part because inflation was under control, which allowed monetary policy to be eased.

Backdrop for First Oil Shock

During the early 1970s the world economy was expanding rapidly. Growth rates in the major industrial countries, which averaged 4 % per annum from 1968 to 1972, surged to 5–6 % in 1972–73. Economic growth in the developing world was even faster.

The rapid expansion resulted in a significant increase in global inflation. In 1973, inflation in the industrial countries averaged nearly 8 %, while that in the developing world was 12 %. The evidence of global inflation was most visible in world commodity prices, which surged by more than 60 %.

Prior to 1973, oil prices were increasing in line with world inflation. However, supply/demand conditions in world oil markets were tightening considerably as a result of increased US dependence on imported oil. The latter was partly fueled by rapid expansion in gasoline consumption and a steady substitution by public utilities from coal to oil. At the same time, domestic oil production in the USA was peaking; yet the Nixon administration imposed price controls on domestically produced oil as part of its wage–price controls program.

As a result, the USA was becoming more dependent on imported oil: After having been self-sufficient in the early 1950s, the USA was importing 35 % of its energy needs in 1973, and US petroleum reserves were nearly depleted. Governments, households and corporations were completely unprepared for what happened in October, when OPEC responded to the US involvement in the Middle East war by imposing an oil embargo that could not be alleviated by increased supply from other sources. Brian Trumbore describes the context as follows:

> The embargo in the U.S. came at a time when 85 % of American workers drove to their places of employment each day… and as gasoline lines snaked their way around blocks and tempers flared (the price at the pump had risen from 30 cents a gallon to about $1.20 at the height of the crisis), conspiracy theories abounded. The rumor with the widest circulation had the whole crisis as being contrived by the major oil importers who were supposedly secretly raking in profits.[1]

Economic Fallout

The impact on the global economy of the quadrupling oil prices and diminished supply of oil was immediate: The major industrial countries were forced to reduce their dependence on imported oil by cutting back on economic output. At the same time, the spike in oil prices sent inflation rates around the world spiraling even higher to double digits.

Central banks responded by tightening monetary policies, which caused aggregate demand to weaken even more. The Federal Reserve, for example, boosted the federal funds rate from 4.5 % in late 1972 to more than 10 % by 1974, while the Bundesbank increased short-term rates by approximately the same amount during 1973. The Bank of Japan raised short-term rates even higher—to 12.5 % by 1974.

Economists at the Council of Economic Advisers calculated that the oil crisis caused declines in real gross domestic product (GDP) of 4.7 % in the USA, 2.5 % in Europe and 7 % in Japan.[2] This translated into what was then the most severe global recession in the post-war era.

At the same time, the surge in oil prices created massive payments imbalances between oil-importing and oil-exporting countries on a scale that had never been imagined. The combined current account surplus of OPEC rose tenfold in 1974 to $67 billion—by far the largest imbalance on record at that time. Policymakers were unsure whether the international financial system would be up to the task of recycling funds from the oil exporters to the oil-importing countries, especially those in the developing world. Unless this group of countries could be offered financial assistance to pay their higher import bills, they would be forced to curtail economic output even more than the industrial countries. Many observers were fearful that the developing countries would have no recourse other than to default on their external debt.

Ameliorating Factors

While the worldwide economic slump from late 1973 to mid-1975 was severe, several developments helped alleviate conditions, such that a worldwide depression was averted. First, policymakers in the major industrial countries and OPEC cooperated to ensure that increased official financing to the developing countries would be forthcoming. A special IMF Oil Facility was created to provide balance-of-payments relief on concessionary terms. Saudi

Arabia, Kuwait and other oil-producing countries also provided increased bilateral assistance to Arab countries.

The vast majority of the financing, however, occurred through multinational banks.[3] They received deposits from OPEC members and, in turn, used the proceeds to lend to the oil-importing countries. This marked a significant change in the pattern of international capital flows: Previously, commercial banks had mainly provided developing countries with short-term trade credits, while official institutions and multilateral lending institutions offered medium- and long-term financing on concessionary terms.

Several factors helped encourage the multinational banks to become involved. First, it was lucrative for them to do so, as they could charge a significant spread over their cost of funding. Second, the developing countries also represented a new source of loan demand, which could help banks to offset weaker loan demand in their home markets. Third, by syndicating loans to medium and smaller banks, the large multinational banks could earn origination fees and also diversify away some of the risk. In addition, the banks effectively could transfer interest rate risk to the borrower by using a short-term interest rate—London Interbank offered rate (LIBOR)—to price the loans.

Crisis Averted

Worries about the financial system abated in 1975 as oil prices stabilized and inflation rates in the industrial countries began to recede. The lessening in inflation enabled the Federal Reserve and other central banks to ease monetary policies. The Federal Reserve, for example, lowered the federal funds rate below 6 % from more than 10 % in 1974. Over this same period, the Bank of Japan reduced its discount rate to 6.5 % from 9 %, while the Bundesbank cut its discount rate in half to 3.5 %. The collective policy actions helped set the stage for a recovery in the industrial world in the second half of the year.

At the same time, the huge payments imbalances between oil exporters and oil importers were reduced significantly, as OPEC's current account surplus was cut in half to $32 billion.[4] This mainly reflected a higher import propensity by OPEC than most forecasters had estimated, as the oil-exporting countries embarked on numerous projects to build infrastructure.

In addition, the oil-importing developing countries were able to maintain reasonably strong growth throughout this period—for two reasons. First, the favorable environment for commodity prices enabled them to enjoy strong export growth. Second, they benefitted from positive resource transfers from abroad as a result of large capital inflows. In this respect, the stepped-up external financing they received from private and official sources helped sustain world economic growth through this difficult transition.

When policymakers of the major industrial countries convened at Rambouillet, France, for their first economic summit, they could breathe a sigh of relief that recycling of petrodollars through the world's financial system proceeded much more smoothly than they had imagined. While a few developing countries were candidates for debt rescheduling, there were no major defaults to rock the world's financial system.

The Interregnum

Over 1976–77, the global economy enjoyed a period of resurgent economic growth, while inflation rates and interest rates trended lower. Investors and policymakers alike were hopeful that the turbulence of the first half of the 1970s was past, and that the global economy could enjoy a more tranquil period ahead. In the USA, there was also a renewed sense of optimism that the acrimony surrounding the Watergate scandal and the Vietnam War would subside, as Jimmy Carter assumed the helm as president.

The calm in financial markets did not last very long, however. During 1977, the US current account swung into a then record deficit (0.5 % of GDP) from a small surplus position in 1976. This shift occurred even though oil prices were softening at the time and OPEC's current account surplus was declining (see Table 3.1). The counterpart, instead, was a tripling in Japan's current account surplus to $11 billion (1.5 % of GDP). As currency traders took note of this development, the dollar came under significant pressure against the yen, falling from about Y300/$ to Y240/$ by year's end. The dollar also weakened considerably against the German mark and Swiss franc in the latter part of the year, as inflation pressures began to resurface: US consumer price inflation averaged 6.5 % in 1977, up from 5.7 % the previous year.

Table 3.1 Current-account positions (billions of dollars)

	USA	Japan	Germany	OPEC	Non-oil less developed countries (LDCs)
1976	4.2	3.7	3.7	37.9	−24.4
1977	−14.5	10.9	4.0	22.2	−21.0
1978	−15.4	16.5	9.2	−2.1	−30.2
1979	0.2	−8.7	−5.5	59.2	−46.3
1980	2.2	−10.7	−13.8	102.4	−71.7

Source: IMF yearbook

The Federal Reserve responded to these developments by raising interest rates gradually, but not enough to compensate for the rise in inflation. At the same time, the US fiscal situation deteriorated, as the federal government began to run budget deficits during a period of strong economic growth. As a result, conditions continued to deteriorate on both the domestic and international fronts in 1978. Inflation accelerated further, ending the year above 8 %, while the current account deficit remained at record levels.

Amid these developments, US economic policymakers came under intense criticism from officials abroad and from investors. Treasury Secretary Michael Blumenthal was criticized for not taking steps to reduce the fiscal imbalance, and he was also accused of favoring a weaker dollar to improve US international price competitiveness. And newly installed Federal Reserve chairman G. William Miller was widely regarded as being too complacent about inflation. Thus, while the Fed raised interest rates under his tenure, the actions typically came in the wake of disappointing news on inflation and trade. As a result, the dollar fell to new lows against the key currencies, and foreign central banks bore the burden of supporting the dollar.

In November, the Carter administration and Federal Reserve acted to restore investor confidence. President Carter indicated that the US government was prepared to intervene heavily in the foreign exchange markets to prop up the dollar, and he announced that the Treasury would issue foreign currency denominated debt for the first time to replenish its foreign exchange reserves. At the same time, the Federal Reserve for the first time in its history boosted the discount rate by a full percentage point to 9.5 %.

By year's end, however, it was unclear whether these actions would turn the tide: At the December meeting of OPEC, the members announced a 15 % increase in the price of oil. The producers stated that they were forced to boost prices because oil demand was escalating and also because the depreciation of the dollar was eroding their purchasing power.

The Second Oil Shock

Any hopes that the US initiatives would bring inflation under control were dashed at the beginning of 1979, when the Shah of Iran was overthrown and Iranian oil production was disrupted. Iran's production plunged from 5.2 million barrels per day (mbd) in late 1978 to only 1.4mbd in 1980, effectively removing 6 % of world production. Oil output fell even further in September 1980, when war broke out between Iraq and Iran.[5]

For the second time in a decade, policymakers and investors again confronted the issue of how the world economy and financial system would cope

Table 3.2 CPI inflation (in %)

	Industrial countries	USA	Japan	Germany	LDCs
1973	7.7	6.2	11.7	5.5	12.2
1974	13.3	11.0	23.1	7.0	16.5
1975	11.2	9.1	11.8	5.9	15.0
1976	8.4	5.7	9.4	4.3	16.0
1977	8.6	6.5	8.2	3.7	16.6
1978	7.3	7.6	4.1	2.7	15.2
1979	9.3	11.3	3.8	4.1	25.0
1980	12.0	13.5	7.8	5.4	28.9

Source: IMF yearbook

with a shortfall in oil. The immediate impact was to produce a tripling in oil prices to $35–$40 per barrel and a massive increase in payments imbalances between OPEC and the oil-importing countries. OPEC's combined current account balance, for example, swung from a small deficit in 1978 to a surplus of $60 billion in 1979. At the peak in 1980, OPEC's surplus was running at an annual rate of $110 billion—nearly two times greater than in the first oil shock.[6]

The main concern for policymakers was to combat inflation, which accelerated to double digits in the industrial countries and even higher rates in the developing world (see Table 3.2). Central banks responded by raising interest rates in order to slow aggregate demand, which had been expanding at a 4 % rate in the industrial world. While this contributed to a slowing of economic activity in 1979, the world economy did not slide into recession, and it even reaccelerated in 1980. Yields on treasuries, which closed out the 1970s near 11 %, climbed to a record high of 13.5 % as investor confidence waned.

The ability of the global economy to withstand higher oil prices and interest rates left many observers optimistic that the recycling of petrodollars would proceed as smoothly as it did during the first shock. However, economists at the World Bank were concerned that the global economy would have to live with even higher oil prices in the future, and that this would imply massive payments imbalances for years to come. Indeed, many investors also concluded that high oil prices and high inflation had become a permanent feature of the world economy.

Oil Shocks: Then and Now

One issue that investment professionals regularly face and that leaves many people perplexed is "market ambiguity." This term describes situations where underlying economic conditions appear to be similar, but the markets' response is different. One reason is that events rarely play out exactly the same, and investment professionals must try to understand what the key differences are and why they matter.

In the case of the first two oil shocks, the circumstances appeared to be very similar. Both involved oil supply disruptions that occurred when the global economy was expanding rapidly and oil demand was strong. Policymakers focused on tackling the inflationary impact of these shocks, because they added to already existing price pressures. These developments, in turn, contributed to a surge in bond yields in both instances.

However, the US stock market response differed substantially: Following the first oil shock, the value of US equities dropped by more than 40 %, whereas the stock market surged by nearly 30 % in 1979–80. Part of the reason is that investors regained confidence that US monetary policy under Fed Chairman Paul Volcker was committed to fight inflation and support the dollar (this is examined in Chap. 4). Indeed, during the decade of the 1980s, prices of oil and other commodities fell steadily from their peaks.

Since the early 1990s, there have been two additional bouts of surging oil prices that were triggered by the threat of supply disruptions. Both were associated with US wars with Iraq, and both times oil prices surged in anticipation of a conflict. When the US economy weakened the Federal Reserve responded by easing monetary policy. Oil prices subsequently softened when it became clear that the military outcome would not result in permanent supply disruptions, and the impact of the oil price increases on financial markets proved to be fleeting.

An additional bout occurred in 1999–2000, when oil prices tripled after having fallen to a low of $10 per barrel in late 1998. Unlike the other episodes, this price increase mainly resulted from strong global demand associated with a tech-led investment boom. OPEC was unwilling to boost output to match the increased demand, and prices continued to climb until the US economy slipped into mild recession in 2001.

In reviewing these experiences, it is evident that the economic impact of successive oil shocks has become progressively less inflationary and also less disruptive to global growth. Accordingly, the impact on financial markets has become more transitory. In this regard, Roger Kubarych has offered the following perspective:

In part, it is because rightly or wrongly market participants have been conditioned to expect the oil price to retreat after a temporary overshoot. And in part it is because a sharp rise in energy costs has differential effects on different sectors of the economy – some industries do worse, such as automobile makers, but others do better, such as energy developers.[7]

My own perspective is that the first two oil shocks were damaging to the global economy, because they accompanied a broad-based rise in global inflation and world interest rates. By comparison, subsequent oil price increases occurred when global inflation was low or falling; hence, investors viewed them as a shift in *relative* prices.

Conclusions

The first two oil shocks marked the first time the US economy was subjected to disruptive shocks from abroad that contributed to "economic stagflation"—a combination of rising inflation and unemployment amid severe recessions. However, some of the adverse consequences on the global economy were diminished by the ease with which funds were recycled from surplus to deficit countries via the international banking system.

Diagnosis of the Problem
The conventional view at the time was that the first oil shock was an exogenous development caused by political turmoil in the Middle East. Accordingly, many economists and policymakers viewed it as temporary. By the end of the decade, however, the second oil shock and accompanying rebound in commodity prices settled the debate and caused investors and policymakers to view high inflation as becoming entrenched.

Policy Response
While higher oil prices tend to dampen output because they constitute a "tax" on consumers, policymakers focused on the broader surge in commodity prices and the acceleration in consumer price inflation that ensued, and monetary policies were tightened significantly. This contributed to a severe recession in 1973–74, which lessened inflation pressures temporarily and enabled monetary policy to be eased. Monetary policy, however, had to be tightened to a much greater extent in the wake of the second oil shock, when investors lost confidence in the ability of policymakers to bring inflation under control.

Market Response
Financial markets gyrated considerably in the 1970s amid large fluctuations in inflation rates and the value of the dollar. For the most part, however, the US operated in the crisis zone of a weak currency, rising bond yields and a shaky stock market.

Table 3.3 Compound annual returns in % (1970s)

	Nominal	Real
Bonds		
LT corporate	6.2	−1.2
LT government	5.5	−1.9
Medium-term gov't	7.0	−0.4
Treasury bills	6.3	−1.1
Equities		
Large cap	5.9	−1.5
Small cap	11.5	4.1
Commodities		
Non-oil	10.3	2.9
Oil	30.1	22.7
Gold	26.9	19.5

Source: IMF yearbook

Portfolio Positioning

Table 3.3 shows the return profile for financial assets and commodities in the 1970s on a compound annual basis. Returns for US bonds averaged 5.5 % to 7.0 % per annum, reflecting high coupon rates at the time. Adjusted for inflation, however, bond returns were negative. In contrast to conventional wisdom at the time, equities provided only a partial hedge against inflation: Returns for large cap stocks were negative by about 1.5 % after adjusting for inflation, although returns for small cap stocks were considerably better. By far, the best performing asset classes were commodities, especially oil and gold. Thus, investors at the time concluded that the best strategy in an inflationary context was to be in real assets rather than financial assets.

Note: Assessing the Impact of Recent Oil Price Declines

This chapter focused on the impact that the first two oil shocks had on the US and global economy, which resulted in rising bond yields and severe recessions on both occasions. Subsequent oil price spikes in the early 1990s and mid-2000s were also associated with recessions, but were not accompanied by rising inflation or higher bond yields. In Table 3.4 we show that, prior to 2014, there were two episodes of steep oil price declines in 1986 and the late 1990s that were accompanied by strong economic growth. This pattern of economic performance is consistent with the notion that oil price declines are tantamount to tax cuts for households and businesses, whereas oil price spikes are comparable to tax hikes.

Table 3.4 Impact of large changes in oil prices on the US economy

Period	Magnitude	Economic impact
Price spikes		
1973–74	Quadrupling	Severe recession
1979–80	Quadrupling	Severe recession
1990–91	Doubling	Mild recession
2006–08	Doubling	Recession (pre-Lehman)
Price declines		
1986	–67 %	Strong growth
1997–98	–60 %	Strong growth
2014–16	–70 %	Moderate growth

Source: IMF

On this basis many economists, including myself, were optimistic that the steep decline in oil prices that began in mid-2014 and continued into early 2016 would bolster the US economy. This has not been the case, however, and the US stock market and high yield bond market have come under pressure, especially as oil prices fell towards $30 per barrel, which many experts regard as being unsustainable over the long term.

This development begs the question: "Why haven't the recent price declines been beneficial to the economy?" My answer is that a key change has occurred in the period since 2008, when US production of oil was running at a rate of 5mbd, to the current situation in which oil production has nearly doubled to more than 9mbd. This increase is a consequence of the revolution in shale oil production, which has enabled the USA to move closer to self-sufficiency in energy. In these circumstances the benefits to consumers from lower oil prices must be netted against the losses that domestic oil producers have sustained, such that the net benefit is considerably smaller than in the past. According to UBS Economic Research, for example, consumer savings on gasoline expenditure in 2015 were $115 billion compared with a decline in energy investment of about $71 billion.[8] The net benefit to the economy of $44 billion is equivalent to less than 3 % of GDP.

For the time being, financial markets are more fixated on the potential losers from falling prices than the potential winners, mainly because the costs borne by producers are material for them: Earnings of oil producers in the USA, for example, are expected to decline in 2016 for the first time since earnings data has been compiled on the sector. At the same time, the high yield bond market is pricing in a rise in default rates for energy issuers in the vicinity of 20 %. Nonetheless, while markets have reacted to the plunge in oil prices as a negative development, one should not forget the long-term benefit to households and companies that are not energy related. These benefits will continue to accrue over time, although they will also be more widely disbursed than the costs that energy producers incur.

Finally, another long-term benefit is that the shale oil revolution has left the USA less dependent on foreign sources of energy. As such, this development lessens the risk that an oil shock from abroad will lead to a US recession.

Notes

1. Brian Trumbore, "The Arab Oil Embargo of 1973–74," Stocks and News. com, July 3, 2003.
2. Council of Economic Advisors, *Economic Report of the President* (Washington, DC: U.S. Government Printing Office, 1981), p. 183.
3. See "Oil Exporters Surpluses and Their Deployment", Bank of England *Quarterly Bulletin*, March 1985, pp. 69–74.
4. Ibid., p. 67.
5. Philip K.Verleger, Jr., "Third Oil Shock: Real or Imaginary?" published by Institute for International Economics, Washington, D.C., April 2000, p. 3.
6. Bank of England, *Quarterly Bulletin*, p. 69.
7. Roger Kubarych, "How Oil Shocks Affect Markets," *The International Economy*, summer 2005.
8. Maury Harris, UBS, December 2015.

4

Anti-Inflation Policies: Intended and Unintended Consequences

US economic policies underwent a shift of seismic proportions from late 1979 through the early 1980s. The Federal Reserve, under Chairman Paul Volcker, redirected monetary policy away from targeting interest rates to controlling money supply as a means of conquering inflation. At the same time, the Reagan administration sought to revitalize the US economy by reducing the size and influence of government and by redirecting resources to the private sector through major reductions in marginal tax rates, government spending and government regulation.

Investors at the time had to discern what impact these policy changes would have on the US economy and on financial markets. Yet there was little to guide policymakers in implementing these changes. Volcker's recollections on the experience acknowledged that the Fed had to improvise at times, because policymakers were unsure how households and businesses would react to higher interest rates. And the Reagan administration had to tolerate increases in government spending in order to win Congressional support for its program of tax cuts.

It was apparent early on that this mix of policies would result in higher US interest rates. But it was far from clear as to how long interest rates would have to stay high before the US economy weakened. And few observers at the time envisioned the impact that these policies would have on developing countries, which were especially vulnerable to higher US interest rates and a strong dollar and, ultimately, unable to meet their debt obligations. Indeed, it was only by the end of the 1980s that a plan was in place to restore the creditworthiness of developing countries.

© The Editor(s) (if applicable) and The Author(s) 2016
N.P. Sargen, *Global Shocks*, DOI 10.1007/978-3-319-41105-7_4

I witnessed these developments while I was an international economist at the Morgan Guaranty Trust Company, where my responsibilities included developing a framework for assessing the ability of countries to service their external debt. In 1983 I was also asked to join a delegation of Morgan officials who worked with counterparts at Deutsche Bank to ensure that commercial banks would roll over existing obligations of developing countries that were experiencing debt problems.

The Volcker Shift in Monetary Policy

President Carter's decision to appoint Paul Volcker as Chairman of the Federal Reserve in July 1979 was part of a cabinet reshuffling in which G. William Miller, the former chairman, replaced Michael Blumenthal as treasury secretary. As US inflation surged to 13 % following the second oil shock, the Carter administration's economic team was divided over economic policy. Blumenthal advocated higher interest rates to bring inflation under control, while Miller was more concerned about the economy.

With US financial markets selling off and the dollar sinking against the key European currencies, the President looked to a man who could restore investor confidence. Historian Charles Geisst made the following observation about Paul Volcker's selection:

> Volcker was selected because he was the candidate of Wall Street. This was their price, in effect. What was known about him? That he was able and bright and it was also known that he was conservative. What wasn't known was that he was going to impose some very dramatic changes.[1]

As Volcker assumed the helm at the Fed, his main priority was to end the spiral of accelerating inflation that had contributed to surging bond yields and a chronically weak dollar. To restore confidence in the conduct of US monetary policy, he needed to convince investors that he was breaking away from the policy of gradualism that had been pursued previously.

Volcker began his tenure audaciously by increasing the discount rate a full percentage point to 13 %, while also announcing a change in the Fed's operating procedures: Instead of setting a target for the federal funds rate, the Fed would henceforth target the growth of bank reserves, which would influence the monetary aggregates. This meant that the Fed was prepared to allow the federal funds rate to rise to the level that would clear the demand for bank reserves.

The main uncertainty was how high the funds rate would rise to clear the market. During the 1960s and early 1970s, the US economy proved to be very sensitive to small increases in the funds rate, because banks and savings and loans faced regulatory ceilings (Reg Q) on deposit rates in order to attract funds. As inflows into these institutions dried up, they were increasingly constrained in making new loans to households or corporations, and the economy weakened. In the wake of the first oil shock, however, the regulatory ceilings were eased in order to sustain the economy. The shift to aggregate reserve targeting, therefore, provided the first opportunity to test how interest-rate resilient the US economy was when banks no longer were subject to disintermediation.

To the amazement of market participants and policymakers alike, short-term interest rates quickly surged to 20 % and higher—levels never before imagined (see Fig. 4.1). In reflecting back on the experiment 22 years later, Volcker observed:

> I do not think that any of us embarking on this policy felt we were going to end up with bank lending rates at 21 percent in the United States. I think that happened because people dependent on bank lending did not follow a nice conceptual textbook approach and say, "the interest rate is a little higher, and so we'll

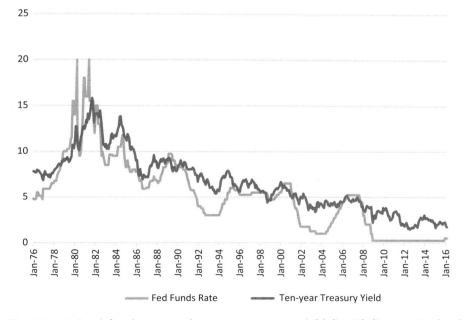

Fig. 4.1 Federal funds rate and ten-year treasury yield (in %) (Source: Federal Reserve, US Treasury)

pull back a little bit." They were caught up in ongoing operations; they were caught up in planned investment programs; they were caught up in their habitual methods of operation. So they kept borrowing and implicitly thinking "well, this interest rate is awfully high today, but maybe it will come down tomorrow, so we'll keep at it." And the credit expansion continued until, to exaggerate a little bit, this became a policy of restraint by bankruptcy.[2]

Amid these developments, investors confronted yet another surprise in 1980, when the Carter administration in conjunction with the Fed imposed controls to limit usage of consumer credit. This experiment was quickly abandoned, however, when consumers stopped spending and the economy plunged into recession. Reflecting on this experiment, Volcker comments:

> We designed what we thought was a modest, market-mimicking restraint on some parts of consumer credit. This was something we anticipated would have a modest restraining effect on the economy, supplementing our control over reserves. It turned out to have a huge psychological effect. I never saw anything like it. There was a sharp reaction by consumers that single-handedly drove the economy into recession in a matter of weeks. I believe that was the last time there was any experimentation in direct control of credit.[3]

Once credit controls were eliminated, interest rates surged once again, after having plummeted temporarily. From 1980 to mid-1982, interest rates were extraordinarily volatile, as market participants awaited the release of weekly money supply data every Thursday at 4:30 p.m. If the money supply approached or exceeded the Fed's targeted ceiling levels, interest rates would surge to bring money growth back in line with the Fed's targets; alternatively, rates would plummet when the monetary aggregates approached or fell below the lower boundaries.

The attention that market participants paid to the money supply data indicated they took the Fed's commitment seriously. However, it remained to be seen how effective the new policy would be in reducing inflation and inflation expectations. By 1981, inflation was still running in double digits, and there was little to indicate that inflation expectations were receding.

Reaganomics

In addition to a sea-change in monetary policy, investors also had to contend with the most comprehensive overhaul of economic policy since the New Deal following Ronald Reagan's election as president in November 1980. Reagan campaigned for office on the theme that reduction in the role of government was key to revitalizing the US economy. The Carter administration was vulnerable, because the so-called "misery index"—the sum of the US unemployment rate and inflation rate—stood at a record 17 % on the eve of the election.

The 1981 Program for Economic Recovery had four major policy objectives: (1) reduce the growth of government spending; (2) lower the marginal tax rates on income both for labor and capital; (3) diminish government regulation; and (4) reduce inflation by controlling the growth of money supply. These policy changes, in turn, were expected to increase saving and investment, boost economic growth, balance the budget, and bolster US financial markets and the dollar, while reducing inflation and interest rates.

The crux of Reaganomics was a belief in "supply side" economics. The central idea was that economic agents—households and businesses—would respond significantly to reductions in marginal tax rates and government regulations by boosting output and incomes. Accordingly, the administration's top priority was to lower personal and corporate tax rates: During its two terms, the Reagan administration reduced the top marginal tax rate on individual income from 70 % to 28 %, while the corporate income tax rate was lowered from 48 % to 34 %.

Proponents of supply-side economics believed that the cuts in marginal tax rates would be self-financing. That is, the tax cuts would stimulate economic activity sufficiently to generate increases in tax revenues. Officials in the Reagan administration also believed that tax cuts would restrain Congress from increasing spending. The administration, however, did not succeed in curbing government spending, which remained in the vicinity of 22–23 % of gross domestic product (GDP). The principal reason was that President Reagan sought significant increases in defense spending, and was unable to convince Congress to offset this via reduced outlays on entitlements and social programs. The tax cuts and expanded outlays, in turn, contributed to large budget deficits that rose from between 2–3 % of GDP in the early 1980s to 5 % of GDP in the mid-1980s.

Impact of Policy Mix on Financial Markets

Investors at the time were unsure how the mix of expansionary fiscal policy and restrictive monetary policy would impact the US and world economy. The impact on interest rates was apparent fairly early: US bond yields soared to record highs, both in nominal and real terms. Yields on ten-year treasuries, for example, surged to 14 % in 1981 (Fig. 4.1), while core inflation hovered around 10 %. Short-term interest rates and the prime lending rate rose well above long-term rates, as the yield curve became steeply inverted—the London Interbank offered rate (LIBOR) reached 20 % and the prime rate rose as high as 22 %.

The spike in US interest rates had one desirable effect from the standpoint of US policymakers. It caused the US dollar to surge against the key currencies, as investors became convinced that the Federal Reserve and the Reagan administration were committed to end the period of dollar weakness. Foreign investors also began to invest in US treasuries, attracted by the combination of high interest rates and an appreciating dollar.

Interest rates peaked in mid-1981 and fell steadily in the second half of the year, amid signs that the economy and inflation were slowing. Many observers at the time believed that recession was imminent. However, interest rates subsequently rebounded when the US economy proved to be surprisingly resilient. Households and corporations continued to borrow at high interest rates to maintain spending, because they believed inflation would stay high, and they also received tax breaks on their borrowing. The elimination of interest rate ceilings also meant that banks could attract deposits at high interest rates to finance loan expansion.

Fed officials were concerned that inflation expectations remained too high, and in spring 1982 they contemplated additional monetary tightening. However, when subsequent data indicated that aggregate demand was weakening and unemployment was rising, the Fed left monetary policy unchanged. By summer, it was becoming apparent to investors that the economy finally was succumbing to high interest rates and was sliding into recession.

Bank Lending to Developing Countries

Following the second oil shock, developing countries continued to be major recipients of syndicated bank loans.[4] Money center banks were willing to lend to these countries, because they earned high spreads over their cost of finance. The experience after the first oil shock also left banks confident that the developing countries could service their debt obligations. The recycling of petrodollars through the international banks is apparent from the massive increase in cross-border bank lending to non-banks: The level rose sevenfold from 1973 to 1982, when it surpassed $700 billion. This was accompanied by nearly a tenfold increase in Latin American debt outstanding by the mid-1980s to about $500 billion.[5]

Table 4.1 Total external debt and debt indicators, 1982 (US$ in billions)

	Total debt	Debt/exports (%)	Debt service ratio (%)
Latin America			
Argentina	43.6	447	50
Brazil	93.0	396	81
Chile	17.3	336	71
Colombia	10.3	204	30
Mexico	86.0	311	57
Peru	10.7	256	49
Venezuela	32.2	160	30
Asia			
Indonesia	24.7	116	18
Korea	37.3	132	22
Malaysia	13.4	93	11
Philippines	24.6	298	43
Thailand	12.2	130	21

Source: Pearson Education, Foreign Debt and Financial Crises, Chap. 11

The accompanying build-up in debt left the developing countries more vulnerable to adverse developments. By the early 1980s, for example, the key borrowers had debt service ratios (interest and amortization on external debt relative to exports of goods and services) well beyond the 20 % threshold that had previously been considered excessive (Table 4.1). Bank economists and analysts who were responsible for country risk appraisal contended that the old rules of thumb were not applicable to countries that had ready access to capital. However, they did not consider what could happen if these countries were suddenly denied access to capital.

Bankers took comfort that policymakers in the industrial countries were encouraging the financial institutions to lend to these countries to mitigate the risk of world recession. And, in the event that problems should arise, these countries could always turn to the International Monetary Fund (IMF) and the World Bank for assistance, as well as to bilateral lending institutions. In one of the more memorable comments at the time, Walter Wriston, Chairman of Citibank, remarked that no sovereign borrower had ever gone bankrupt.

The result was the major money center banks permitted their exposure to these countries to rise to levels well beyond what was prudent. By the early 1980s, for example, the exposures of the major money center banks to the four largest Latin American borrowers (Argentina, Brazil, Mexico and Venezuela) ranged between 100–200 % of their capital.

The Developing Country Debt Crisis

The news in early August of 1982 that Mexico had run out of foreign exchange reserves and was seeking stand-by credits from the IMF stunned the international financial community. Soon after, the other principal Latin American borrowers—Brazil, Argentina and Venezuela—were also seeking debt relief. The four countries owed various commercial banks $176 billion—approximately three-quarters of the total debt outstanding in the less developed countries (LDCs) —of which about $37 billion was owed to the eight largest US banks and constituted nearly 150 % of their capital and reserves at the time.[6]

The multinational banks and policymakers in the industrial countries were caught completely off guard by these developments. When I returned from vacation in early September, my boss, Rimmer De Vries told me he had never seen senior management so worried about the possibility of major losses on loans to the key Latin American borrowers. As the situation unfolded, the senior management of Morgan Guaranty asked our department first to assess what had gone wrong, and then how serious the problem was. Some participants—notably the chief lending officers for the problem countries—maintained they faced a liquidity shortage that could be alleviated by a combination of IMF assistance and short-term bank financing. However, our department concluded that the problems were more serious and would require coordinated action among banks, developing countries and official institutions to prevent a collapse of the international financial system.

The factors contributing to the problems were fairly easy to diagnose after the fact. First, the debt service burdens of the borrowers were considerably greater than after the first oil shock because of the build-up in debt that occurred and the much higher interest rates (and US dollar) that prevailed in the early 1980s. Second, the ensuing recession in the US and industrial world caused commodity prices to plummet, making it more difficult for the borrowers to earn the foreign exchange to service their external debt. Third, as the banks became aware of the problem, they were reluctant to extend new credits to these countries, such that their access to capital dried up.

A key factor that complicated the assessment of the situation was the lack of comprehensive and timely information on the external debt of the developing countries. The principal source of data compiled by the World Bank covered borrowing from official sources with original maturities of more than one year, and the most recent information was two years old. As more up-to-date information was compiled from the problem countries, it soon became apparent that much of their recent borrowing had been from commercial banks on a short-term basis. Banks apparently felt that by keeping countries on a short leash they could easily reduce their exposure if anything went wrong. However, they did not realize that all banks were doing the same thing, which only compounded the situation. Ironically, a system that I developed at the San Francisco Fed in the mid-1970s sent off early warning signals in 1980. However, I thought they were a mistake, because I had incorrectly specified an equation, and therefore chose to ignore them! (I later realized that I was worried of being accused of crying "fire" in a crowded theater, and was afraid to make a wrong call of such magnitude.)

Policy Easing

Once the enormity of the problem was understood, policymakers in the industrial countries had to ensure that banks did not collectively pull funds out of the developing countries. To do so would leave the borrowers with little choice other than to default on their debt.

At the IMF-World Bank meetings in September, officials, bankers and representatives from the developing countries worked on a plan to ensure that existing debt obligations would be extended in return for the borrowing countries agreeing to pursue policies that would reduce their future borrowing needs. Effectively, this meant that the borrowers would allow their currencies to depreciate while they tightened fiscal and monetary policies to reduce their external imbalances. The key money center banks, in turn, were expected to pressure other syndicate members to maintain existing commitments.

For this effort to work, policymakers in the industrial countries needed to act boldly to the end the recession in the industrial world. Recognizing this, the Federal Reserve and other central banks eased monetary policies aggressively, and investors reacted by shifting funds into stocks and bonds. Steven Solomon describes the dramatic shift that Paul Volcker made away from aggregate targeting as follows:

> On June 30 in the midst of the Penn Square crisis and on the very same day the Fed made its second secret overnight loan to Mexico, the FOMC convened for a two-day meeting in an atmosphere of pessimism and gloom. Despite the continued deep slide of the U.S. economy and evidence of fragility, the key monetary aggregates were still rising at the upper end of their long-run ranges.
>
> With every intuition and real economic indicator telling him the United States was on the edge of economic catastrophe, Volcker at last ignored the monetary rule. The FOMC voted for a major easing.[7]

The harsh disinflation squeeze was over. The Fed funds rate plunged from 14 % to 11 % by the end of July. By mid-December it was down to 8.8 %. Between July and December the Fed cut the discount rate seven times. Stock and bond markets soared as investors were emboldened that both inflation and interest rates had peaked. My future boss at Salomon Brothers, Henry Kaufman, helped ignite the rally when he changed his long-standing pessimism about US inflation and supported the Fed's efforts to lower interest rates.

The US and other developed countries recovered from recession in the second half of 1983, and inflation and interest rates both plummeted from the highs reached in the early 1980s. Nonetheless, the cost for ending the inflationary spiral was severe: The 1982–83 recession turned out to be the worst in the post-war era in terms of increases in unemployment rates and declines in capacity utilization rates in the industrial world. Conditions in the third world were fragile, as the developing countries confronted massive debt burdens and net capital outflows.

These developments contributed to significant declines in commodity prices. By 1983, the price of gold was down nearly half from its peak of more than $800 in 1981, while the price of oil fell below $30 per barrel from a peak of nearly $40. At the same time, OPEC's massive current account surplus dwindled as a result of weaker demand for oil and rapid import growth.

Managed Lending and Regulatory Forbearance

While monetary policy easing helped restore economic growth in the developed world by mid-1983, the situation confronting developing economies continued to worsen: By October, 27 countries owing approximately $240 billion had rescheduled their debt to banks or were in the process of doing so.[8] The plan worked out by the governments of the Group of Seven (G-7) in conjunction with the IMF and the leading global financial institutions called for a three-part response: (1) the banks would continue to roll over existing LDC debt obligations; (2) the heavily indebted countries would embark on programs to reduce their external imbalances; and (3) official institutions would fill the remaining gap in new borrowings.[9]

It was evident at the time that the LDCs would not be able to repay their debt obligations. However, the money center banks did not want to call them into default, because it would reveal the fragility of their own balance sheets. Therefore, they preferred to buy time by rolling over LDC debt on favorable terms while valuing the loans on their books at par. To do so, the regulatory bodies overseeing the banks acquiesced by not requiring US banks to set aside large reserves on restructured LDC loans. According to William Seidman, chairman of the Federal Deposit Insurance Corporation (FDIC) at the time, regulatory forbearance was necessary, because seven or eight of the ten largest banks in the US might have been deemed insolvent:

> U.S. bank regulators, given the choice between creating panic in the banking system and going easy on requiring banks to set aside reserves for Latin American debt, had chosen the latter course. It would appear the regulators made the right choice.[10]

This strategy paid off, as no large US bank failed because of delinquency or non-performing loans. However, the money center banks encountered numerous challenges—the most important being that their profitability was impacted by reduced charges on loans outstanding to LDCS and the ability of companies with high credit ratings to obtain cheaper financing in the commercial paper market. At the same time, money center banks constantly had to arm twist regional banks to roll over their portions of the syndicated loans to the debt-troubled countries.

In 1985 Treasury Secretary James Baker offered a formula that called for banks to extend debt repayments over a longer time period, but which did not offer any debt forgiveness. It was predicated on the assumption that debtors could grow their way out of debt and could expand their exports enough to reduce their relative debt burdens to levels compatible with a return to normal credit market access. The Baker Plan, however, encountered major obstacles when LDC growth failed to materialize and the debt-burdened countries grew weary of austerity.

It was not until March 1989 that the US government finally sanctioned the idea of *debt reduction* with a new plan formulated by Treasury Secretary Nicholas Brady. Mexico was the first country to conclude a Brady Plan debt reduction agreement, because it had large debt outstanding, had embarked on an economic reform program and was strategically important to the US. The Brady Plan stipulated that US banks would reduce principal and interest on LDC debt and would receive guarantees on the remaining portion of the debt.[11] These guarantees, in turn, enabled the bank loans to be converted into Brady bonds, which were marketable securities. In this regard, securitization was viewed as a way for banks to get loans they did not want to hold off their balance sheets while the developing countries could take the first step to restoring their access to capital markets.

Unforeseen Developments

The US experience in the early 1980s offers interesting insights into the way that officials, investors and financial markets reacted to a regime shift in the conduct of US monetary and fiscal policies. First, while Fed Chairman Volcker believed "shock therapy" was necessary to convince market participants of the Fed's commitment to control inflation, he and other policymakers were surprised by the volatility of interest rates that ensued. Second, while most economists at the time believed the spike in interest rates would trigger a recession in 1980–81, the economy proved to be more interest-rate resilient than expected, and it did not weaken materially until 1982. Third, the event that shattered inflation expectations was completely unanticipated, when the major LDC borrowers ran out of foreign exchange reserves in August and September. It is a prime example of the "law of unintended consequences."

Finally, prior to the LDC debt crisis, financial markets had been very turbulent in the 1970s and early 1980s, but the soundness of the international financial system was never in question. That perception changed suddenly for money center banks and their regulators when it became apparent they had more loans outstanding to the key borrowers than they had capital. In the end, policymakers and the leading banks were able to agree on a solution, in which banks could hold loans on their balance sheets at par, while they formed a cartel to roll over existing obligations under IMF auspices.

The strategy of "managed lending" effectively bought time for the money center banks to replenish their capital, which enabled them to begin writing down debt by the end of the decade. Because it was successfully implemented, it was not a focal point for investors, who instead focused on the monetary policy easing in the industrial countries, which sparked a rally in financial markets that preceded a powerful recovery in the industrial countries.

It is relevant, however, to consider the counter-factual: What would have happened if there had not been regulatory forbearance?

My answer is that the outcome would have been very different. Had banks been forced to mark the value of their loans to market, banks would have had to de-lever their balance sheets and a credit crunch would have ensued. In such circumstances, recovery in the industrial countries would have been much more subdued and the markets' response far less favorable. My conclusion, therefore, is that the policy response of coordinated monetary policy easing, coupled with regulatory forbearance to the LDC debt crisis, was critical to the outcome.

Finally, it should also be noted that the securitization of developing country debt that began in the late 1980s was instrumental in enabling the debt-burdened countries to regain access to international capital markets in the 1990s. Ironically, two decades later the process of securitizing low-quality mortgages turned out to be the catalyst for the 2008 financial crisis. In this respect, securitization proved to be both a powerful force for resolving the LDC debt crisis and an agent for the global financial crisis.

Conclusions

During the early 1980s US economic policies underwent regime changes as never before, with Paul Volcker's decision to end targeting of the fed funds rate and President Reagan's push to lower marginal tax rates and to lessen regulatory burdens. Amid this, investors faced the difficult task of assessing how these policy shifts would impact the US economy and financial markets.

Diagnosis of the Problem
By the end of the 1970s, it was clear that investors had lost confidence in US economic policies, as the country faced unacceptably high inflation and a chronically weak dollar. Upon becoming Fed Chairman, Paul Volcker was prepared to do whatever was required to bring inflation under control and to restore confidence in the dollar, while President Reagan also wanted to unleash obstacles to strong growth.

Policy Response
Volcker's change in the Fed's operating procedures resulted in real interest rates rising to record levels. This succeeded in stabilizing the dollar, as foreign investors added to holdings of dollar assets. Nonetheless, US bond yields stayed stubbornly high despite evidence that the US economy was weakening. The event that altered inflation expectations irrevocably was the LDC debt crisis, which was completely unforeseen by policymakers and investors. While it could have threatened the solvency of some of the world's largest financial institutions, officials in the G-7 formulated a coordinated policy response to lessen the impact on the global economy, and bank regulators practiced forbearance that gave banks time to grow out of their problems.

Market Response
As investors became convinced that the era of high inflation was over, US stocks and bonds soared in value, while the dollar experienced unprecedented strength.

Portfolio Positioning
The optimal strategy in these circumstances was to go long the dollar and US financial assets, while shorting gold, oil and commodities.

Notes

1. Charles R. Geisst, *Wall Street: A History*, Updated edition, 2012.
2. "Monetary Policy Transmission: Past and Future Challenges," address by Paul A. Volcker to Conference on Financial Innovation and Monetary Transmission, sponsored by the Federal Reserve Bank of New York, April 2002, p. 4.
3. Ibid., p. 4.
4. For an excellent discussion of the events surrounding the LDC debt crisis see, Solomon, *The Confidence Game*.
5. Federal Deposit Insurance Corporation, History of 80s, p. 194.
6. Ibid., p. 191.
7. Solomon, *The Confidence Game*, p. 161.
8. Ibid., p. 191.
9. For further discussion see Nicholas Sargen, "Managed Lending: An Assessment of the Current Strategy toward LDC debt," *NYU Journal of Law and Politics*, Spring 1985.
10. William Seidman, *Full Faith and Credit*, p. 127.
11. During 1990–94, 12 Brady Plan agreements were reached, and there were an additional five more during 1995–97.

5

Policy Coordination Gives Way to Conflict and Turmoil

Do deficits matter? This issue was widely debated in the mid-1980s, when the USA ran large budget and current account deficits (see Fig. 5.1). During the early years of the Reagan administration, investors pretty much ignored the deterioration in the fiscal and external accounts. Most were encouraged that the Federal Reserve was committed to reducing inflation, and they were comforted that the political pendulum was swinging toward market-oriented policies. When Japan displaced the Organization of the Petroleum Exporting Companies (OPEC) as the world's largest capital exporter, the USA was able to attract capital inflows from abroad on favorable terms.

In the mid-1980s, however, concerns about US "twin deficits" increased, especially as the US fiscal and current account deficits exceeded 3 % of gross domestic product (GDP). Critics of the Reagan administration believed the "supply-side" policies it pursued were misguided and would effectively mortgage the country's future, leaving behind a legacy of high interest rates. Other observers, including the Federal Reserve Chairman Paul Volcker, worried that the USA was vulnerable to a shift in international capital flows. For their part, officials in Japan and Europe actively pressed the Reagan administration to take steps to reduce the US imbalances.

No one, however, envisioned the events that would subsequently unfold. From 1985 to 1987, policymakers in the USA, Japan and Europe coordinated their economic policies to engineer a "soft landing" for the dollar. Initially, it appeared they had pulled off a major coup, as investors stayed calm even though the US dollar depreciated much more rapidly than in the 1970s. By 1987, however, it appeared that the Volcker nightmare scenario was unfold-

© The Editor(s) (if applicable) and The Author(s) 2016   **61**
N.P. Sargen, *Global Shocks*, DOI 10.1007/978-3-319-41105-7_5

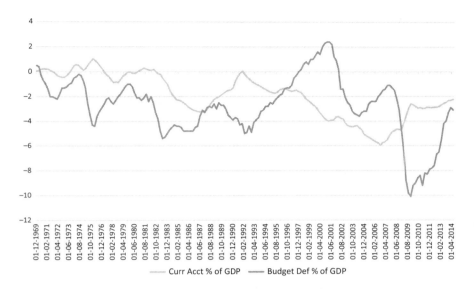

Fig. 5.1 US current-account and budget deficits (% of GDP) (Source: US Treasury, Department of Commerce)

ing, when Japanese and other international investors became alarmed that there was no floor for the dollar. A conflict between US policymakers and their Japanese and German counterparts contributed to the October 1987 stock market crash that many observers at the time believed would herald a global recession.

Budget Deficits and Current Account Deficits

Among the key changes that occurred in the mid-1980s was Japan's emergence as a financial superpower. During the 1970s, Japan's current account shifted into surplus as the country's saving rate outstripped the pace of domestic investment, but rising commodity prices kept the surplus in check. When commodity prices weakened in the early 1980s, Japan's external surplus mushroomed, and it eventually supplanted OPEC as the world's largest capital exporter.

A significant portion of the increase in Japan's external surplus stemmed from a growing bilateral trade surplus with the USA. Japanese manufacturers benefitted from a weakening of the yen in the early 1980s, and their exports to the USA surged as the US economy recovered from recession. Throughout the 1980s, US officials contended that the main reason for the large bilateral trade imbalance was the Japanese government's interventions in currency markets to limit the appreciation of the yen versus the dollar. As a result, US–Japanese trade disputes became more intense in the 1980s.

The Japanese government's response was that the large US current account deficits were caused, in fact, by persistent, large US budget deficits, which it labeled as "twin deficits." The rationale underpinning this argument is based on the accounting identity[1]:

$$M - X = (G - T) + (I - S)$$

This states that a trade imbalance (imports minus exports) is equal to the sum of a budget imbalance (government spending minus taxes) and a saving-investment imbalance in the private sector. If the latter imbalance is unchanged, therefore, a change in the budget deficit is associated with a change in the current account deficit.

Accordingly, the Japanese government (along with European officials) argued that the best way for the USA to narrow its trade imbalance would be to adopt measures to reduce its government budget deficit. However, because the USA did not tackle its budget imbalance until the mid-1990s, the burden of adjustment for narrowing the trade imbalance ultimately was relegated to the yen/dollar exchange rate, which appreciated steadily from 1985 to 1994.

Japan's Emergence as a Financial Power

One consequence of the build-up of Japan's current account surplus was that policymakers needed to liberalize the country's rigid foreign exchange and capital controls. They began to do so in the early 1980s, and the process of liberalization was well under way by the mid-1980s. This process enabled Japanese financial institutions such as life insurance companies, trust banks and commercial banks to invest a larger percentage of their assets in foreign securities. These institutions concentrated most of their purchases in US bonds and, for the most part, they were motivated by the higher yields they could earn on US bonds than on Japanese government bonds.

The significance of Japan's emergence as the world's leading capital exporter is highlighted by a comparison of the disposition of OPEC's external surplus with Japan's.[2] At the peak of OPEC's surplus in the early 1980s, approximately 30 % of the proceeds were invested in the USA. Yet only about $35 billion—or less than 10 % of the surplus—was held in US bonds, with the majority being distributed among international bank deposits, equities and real estate, and direct placements with developing countries. By comparison, Japanese investors overwhelmingly were buyers of international bonds, with the majority being dollar denominated: Holdings of foreign securities rose from less than $20 billion at year end 1979 to nearly $550 billion at year end 1989. Of this total, more than 90 % were foreign bonds, and the vast majority were denominated in dollars.

The heavy concentration of Japanese purchases of dollar-denominated bonds led some observers at the time to assert that Japanese institutions had little choice other than to invest in the USA. This line of reasoning, however, failed to separate *ex ante* and *ex post* considerations. While the US current account deficit ultimately was financed, the relevant consideration was the *terms* on which Japanese or other investors were willing to acquire dollar-denominated assets.

A Resurgent Dollar

During the first term of the Reagan administration, the dollar continued to rise steadily, as Japanese and other international investors helped finance record fiscal and current account deficits that were in the vicinity of 3–4 % of GDP. In the aftermath of the developing country debt crisis, the Federal Reserve monitored money supply growth, but reverted to targeting the federal funds rate. The Fed, however, refrained from monetizing the enlarged budget deficits, such that real interest rates remained unusually high—in the vicinity of 4–6 %—which was attractive to international investors.

Policymakers abroad, however, were concerned that the situation was untenable, and many currency forecasters predicted a collapse of the dollar. Yet the US currency continued to defy the experts.

A key test of the dollar's strength occurred in early 1984, when inflation expectations increased as the US economy posted 5 % growth and commodity prices increased for the first time in several years. The dollar weakened against the key currencies, and interest rates in the USA rose relative to those abroad—an indication that international investors were losing confidence in the dollar. Fed chairman Paul Volcker, who worried the US economy was vulnerable to capital flight, responded forcefully, boosting the discount rate by a full percentage point. The dollar subsequently resumed its upward trend, as commodity prices plummeted on the news and bonds rallied.

During the remainder of 1984, the dollar continued to advance, even as interest rate differentials narrowed between the USA and abroad. The US currency was buttressed by stellar US economic performance and renewed investor confidence that inflation would stay under control. Treasury Secretary Donald Regan, a strong dollar advocate, contended that the currency's strength was a vote of confidence in favor of US economic policies. To make US Treasuries even more attractive to foreign investors, the US government abolished a 10 % withholding tax. This triggered a flood of foreign buying that sent the dollar to new highs.

The Plaza Accord

The Reagan administration's commitment to a strong dollar shifted at the beginning of its second term in January 1985, when James Baker replaced Donald Regan as US Treasury Secretary. The administration was committed to promoting strong economic growth; yet there were increasing signs that the economy was faltering. The reason: US manufacturers were encountering problems competing internationally due to the strong dollar. Consequently, the US trade deficit continued to expand even as the economy softened, heightening protectionist pressures in the USA.

The turn in the dollar occurred in the first quarter of 1985, amid extraordinary volatility in the currency markets. Early in the year, the US Treasury joined in coordinated intervention against the dollar, reversing its former position against exchange market intervention. But the US participation was fairly modest, and the initial foray failed to reverse the dollar's upward thrust. At its peak in late February, the dollar reached DM3.47 and Y265—an appreciation of more than 50 % and 25 %, respectively, from levels at the end of 1978.

This did not deter central bankers, however, who gathered in Basel to negotiate the modalities of a massive, coordinated intervention to alter exchange rate expectations. The Bundesbank, which previously was reluctant to intervene, agreed to play a central role in the effort. This action marked the turning point for the dollar. By late summer, however, the dollar rallied, much to the consternation of policymakers.

At a weekend meeting of finance ministers held at the Plaza Hotel in September, Treasury Secretary Baker stunned the financial markets by announcing that the US government and other Group of Seven (G-7) members agreed to engineer an orderly decline of the dollar. The respective central banks would pursue coordinated intervention, selling dollars for foreign currencies, to achieve this objective. The foreign exchange markets reacted immediately to the news, sending the dollar sharply lower against the major currencies.

While the Plaza Accord succeeded in convincing investors that policymakers wanted a weaker dollar, G-7 officials also had to coordinate monetary policies to ensure that the dollar's decline was orderly. If the Federal Reserve lowered interest rates unilaterally, it could trigger a run on the dollar that would result in higher US bond yields. Therefore, it was essential for the Bank of Japan and the Bundesbank to ease monetary policies, along with the Fed.

The key challenge for G-7 policymakers at the Plaza meeting was whether they could engineer the largest decline of the dollar in history, without triggering a crisis of confidence that would undermine the international financial system. By the end of 1986, it appeared policymakers had pulled off a major coup: The dollar had fallen to Y160 and DM1.95, respectively; at the same time, ten-year Treasury bond yields declined to 7.0 %. A key factor that helped spur the rally in the bond market was a precipitous decline in the price of oil, which helped lower inflation to 2 %.

Policymakers were not completely out of the woods, however, as there were indications that Japanese investors were growing wary about the dollar's steady decline. Because they purchased US bonds without hedging their exposure back into yen, they suffered substantial losses on their currency positions that offset the gains on their bond positions. As a result, they were becoming concerned that the US administration was not doing enough to stabilize the dollar. I was informed by boss Henry Kaufman about this in September 1986, and we discussed the possibility that further dollar weakness could lead to a loss of investor confidence in the dollar.

The Louvre Accord

In early 1987, US bond yields surged as the dollar plummeted further and inflation accelerated when oil prices reversed direction.[3] The bond market suffered a major setback in February, when investors worried that Japanese institutions might pull funds out of the USA if the authorities did not act to halt the dollar's slide.

In order to calm the financial markets, Treasury Secretary Baker agreed to meet with Japanese and European officials at the Louvre in Paris to agree on steps to stabilize the dollar. Baker's primary motive was to head off a significant rise in US interest rates, and he wanted to make sure that foreign central banks would not raise their rates. According to Solomon:

Baker's effort to finesse dollar stabilization at existing U.S. interest rate levels was the source of one of the most controversial secret understandings – or, in actuality, misunderstandings – among many Louvre participants: the presumption that U.S. interest rates would not be raised and, abroad, possibly lowered.[4]

For their part, central banks committed to intervene in the foreign exchange markets, buying dollars and selling currencies, to keep the dollar within the target zones they had set. Currency traders, nonetheless, responded by driving the dollar below these zones, when they sensed that the central banks were reluctant to alter monetary policies to stabilize the dollar. When Japanese investors threatened to boycott the US Treasury quarterly refunding in April, the Fed responded by raising interest rates, and Treasury Secretary Baker advocated support for a stronger dollar.

Market conditions improved in May, when Japanese investors actively participated in the Treasury refunding. However, this required considerable pressure from Japanese authorities:

> The downward pressure on the dollar finally abated only after the Japanese MOF applied strong administrative guidance a week later. On May 13 the heads of ten securities firms, twenty banks, ten insurance companies, and fifteen foreign banks were called in and warned about the repercussions of speculating against the dollar.[5]

These actions helped calm the financial markets temporarily. However, the dollar came under renewed pressure in August, when the USA continued to post large trade deficits and inflation accelerated. This triggered a further sell-off in the bond market.

The October 1987 Stock Market Crash

Throughout this period, the US stock market was surprisingly resilient to the surge in US interest rates and decline in the dollar. For the most part, equity investors focused on improving corporate profits, and chose to ignore the turmoil in the bond and currency markets.

In August, however, the stock market came under selling pressure, especially when Paul Volcker announced he was stepping down as Chairman of the Fed. His successor, Alan Greenspan, was highly regarded, but investors were unsure about his credentials as an inflation fighter and immediately tested his resolve. In his first act as chairman, Greenspan pressed for a 50 basis point hike in interest rates in order to reassure investors.

Normally this action would have calmed the financial markets. However, market volatility increased in September, when the Bank of Japan and the Bundesbank both nudged short-term interest rates higher. Treasury Secretary Baker considered this to be a violation of the Louvre Accord, and tensions mounted between US officials and policymakers in Japan and Germany.

By mid-October, US financial markets were in turmoil, as G-3 policymakers bickered openly about what needed to be done to restore confidence in the dollar. On Monday, October 19, press reports indicated that Treasury Secretary Baker no longer favored currency intervention to support the dollar, and the currency was in near free-fall. Treasury bond yields surged by 50 basis points to 10.5 %, and the stock market opened down 200 points in the morning. The stock market continued to gyrate wildly during the day, and closed down more than 500 points for a 23 % decline. This, in turn, contributed to a worldwide stock market rout.

For some observers, this was the nightmare situation they had dreaded, in which the USA's vulnerability to international capital flows was exposed. To calm the situation, Fed Chairman Greenspan announced that the Fed stood ready to supply whatever liquidity was needed, and it subsequently eased monetary policy. The Bank of Japan and Bundesbank also added liquidity to the markets, as policymakers quickly patched up their differences. Investors then had to assess whether the huge decline in equity prices would cause a worldwide recession, or whether the monetary policy actions could stabilize the situation.

1988 Surprises

While the central bank policy actions helped stabilize the US and world equity markets, investors were nervous that markets could go back into a tailspin if the dollar came under renewed pressure. The reason: Capital outflows from Japan dried up after Black Monday and did not begin flowing again until early 1988. Stephen Solomon points out the key role that the central banks played in supporting the financial markets throughout the turbulence of 1987:

> Central bankers' substitution for fleeing private global investors helped save the plummeting dollar from Volcker's nightmarish free-fall and hard economic landing... The unprecedented 1987 central bank dollar intervention amounted to another of the atypical rescues that were becoming more commonplace with

the rise of global capital. For all of 1987 central bankers acquired a record $120 billion in assets. Effectively they financed almost two-thirds of the foreign borrowing needs for the year.[6]

For its part, the Federal Reserve under Chairman Greenspan deployed a strategy of holding interest rates low to avoid recession, while also seeking to reassure international investors of the commitment to support the dollar. At the start of 1988, most forecasters believed the US was close to recession, with the index of leading economic indicators falling for four consecutive months. Monetarists such as Beryl Sprinkel, the Chairman of the Council of Economic Advisors, were particularly worried, because money supply growth had fallen far short of the Fed's stated targets.

At the same time, central bankers in Europe and Japan began to worry that the efforts to support the dollar could reignite the inflation fears prior to the stock market sell-off. The Japanese economy proved to be surprisingly resilient, and the economies of Europe were experiencing an investment boom. By February, assessments of the US economy also began to shift, as economic indicators turned out much stronger than expected. And by late March, the economy was sufficiently resilient for the Fed to begin raising interest rates again.

International Capital Flow Dynamics

Looking back on the experience of the 1980s is particularly useful for understanding the dynamics of international capital flows. While at Salomon Brothers, John Lipsky and I developed a framework that uses information about international capital flows to study changes in the relationship between interest rate differentials (or yield spreads) and exchange rates. The key relationship is the tendency for interest rate parity to hold along the yield curve. At any point in time, arbitrageurs will ensure that the forward premium or discount for a currency is equal to the interest rate differential. The challenge for global investors is to understand what the driving forces are, while also recognizing that the primary drivers may change over time.

This concept is illustrated in the quadrant diagram that was presented in Chap. 1 and that is shown in Fig. 5.2 , in which the vertical axis measures interest rate differentials (US minus foreign) and the horizontal axis measures exchange rate changes. The first and third quadrants depict situations in which monetary policy developments are the principal forces driving currency movements, and are typically covered in economics and finance textbooks.

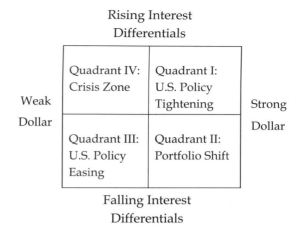

Fig. 5.2   Interest rate differentials and the dollar

The second and fourth quadrants, however, illustrate situations that are often associated with changes in inflation expectations or shifts in asset preferences. In these situations, expectations about currencies drive yield spreads. For instance, the fourth quadrant, or "crisis zone," illustrates a situation in which expectations about dollar depreciation may cause investors to require a larger interest rate premium to hold dollar-denominated assets.

An intriguing feature of this approach is the pattern of quadrant shifts that occurred in the 1980s, in which there was a clockwise rotation around the four quadrants. There is no *a priori* reason why this rotation must prevail, but it seems to result from the responses of policymakers and international investors to business-cycle and inflation developments.

The easiest situations to grasp are those in which the dollar responded primarily to changes in US monetary policy. For example, the tight monetary policy in the early 1980s and again in the late 1980s was aimed at fighting inflation. In both instances, this action induced capital flows that contributed to dollar appreciation (Quadrant I). Conversely, because of a weakening of the US economy and an excessively strong dollar, the Federal Reserve eased policy, and the US bond market rallied while the dollar plunged (Quadrant III).

Dollar crises (Quadrant IV)—in which US interest rates rose as the dollar fell—are more difficult to forecast, because they entail a loss of investor confidence. Foreign exchange rate crises, however, typically are resolved by a predictable outcome—policy tightening, with the principal uncertainty being the timing of the action. The most difficult situations to anticipate were those in which the dollar appreciated while US interest rates fell (Quadrant II).

This occurred in 1984 when capital inflows surged as inflation expectations diminished and investors anticipated capital gains from holding US bonds. In light of these considerations, one can understand why econometric studies of capital flows had a poor track record: They were developed to explain stable relationships such as Quadrants I and III, but it is much more difficult to model shifts in inflation expectations or in asset preferences, such as in Quadrants II and IV.

Lessons Learned from Disinflation

The experience of the 1980s is especially relevant for investors because it highlights two key sets of forces at play: (1) the US monetary policy regime shift in the early 1980s succeeded in bringing inflation under control but at the expense of a severe recession and developing country debt crisis; while (2) the policies of the Reagan administration succeeded in spurring the US economy by lowering marginal tax rates, but they failed to rein in large US budget and current account deficits that contributed to trade disputes.

Amid these developments, there were several interesting surprises for investors:

- First, contrary to popular impression at the time, large US budget and current account deficits turned out to be compatible with falling bond yields. The reason: These imbalances contributed to high real interest rates; however, the principal drivers of declining bond yields were monetary policies that succeeded in lowering inflation expectations.
- Second, the US dollar and the British pound appreciated materially in the first half of the decade despite twin deficits, mainly because high real interest rates and falling inflation expectations attracted massive capital inflows. The respective overshoots of these currencies as measured by deviations from purchasing power parity (PPP) were the largest in the era of flexible exchange rates. In both instances, policymakers ultimately had to ease monetary policy to correct the overshoot.
- Third, worries that "twin deficits" left the USA vulnerable to capital flight surfaced on several occasions, but the worst outcome—the "Volcker nightmare"—did not materialize. Nonetheless, on several occasions, coordinated policy responses of the G-7 were required to stabilize financial markets. More recently, worries about possible capital flight from the USA resurfaced in the past decade when China supplanted Japan as the world's largest capital exporter.

- Fourth, while the 1980s highlighted the important influence of international capital flows, investors also learned some valuable lessons about the impact of disinflation on financial markets. The most obvious is that *disinflation was very positive for financial assets, which materially outperformed commodities in the 1980s, as well as the 1990s* (Table 5.1).

Finally, what is particularly intriguing about the decade of the 1980s is that it represented the high-water mark in terms of efforts by G-7 officials to coordinate policies to stabilize financial markets. Thus, while currency markets remained volatile in the ensuing decades, efforts at policy coordination waned considerably until the 2008 global financial crisis. Part of the reason is that subsequent declines in the dollar proved to be "benign" in that they were typically accompanied by declines in US interest rates. Instead, a new phenomenon—"asset price inflation"—surfaced, beginning in Japan in the late 1980s. The experience of asset bubbles, in turn, would pose a new set of challenges for policymakers and investors alike in the 1990s and 2000s.

Conclusions

Diagnosis of Problem

The US dollar had become excessively strong as a result of massive capital inflows that were induced by high real interest rates and the Reagan administration's endorsement of a strong currency. The administration shifted its

Table 5.1 Compound annual returns in % (1980s and 1990s)

	1980s		1990s	
	Nominal	Real	Nominal	Real
Bonds				
L T corp	13.0	7.9	8.4	5.5
L T gov't	12.6	7.5	8.8	5.9
Med-term gov't	11.0	5.9	7.2	4.3
Treasury Bills	8.9	3.8	4.9	2.0
Equities				
Large cap	17.6	12.5	18.2	15.3
Small cap	15.8	10.7	15.1	12.2
Commodities				
Oil	−9.3	−14.4	1.6	−1.3
Gold	−2.4	−7.5	−3.3	−6.2

Source: Ibbotson Associates, 2003 Yearbook; IMF Yearbook

stance in 1985, however, when the US economy slowed because US companies were encountering difficulties competing internationally. The challenge that policymakers faced was to develop a strategy that would produce a substantial depreciation of the dollar without undermining investor confidence.

Policy Response

Policymakers in the major industrial countries realized they would have to coordinate monetary policies to achieve the desired outcome. Under the Plaza Accord, central bankers engaged in coordinated intervention in currency markets and monetary policy easing in order to guide the dollar and US interest rates lower. The Louvre Accord, by comparison, sought to stabilize the dollar via monetary policy tightening by the Federal Reserve and policy easing by the Bundesbank and Bank of Japan.

Market Response

The Plaza Accord proved very successful in achieving its objectives, and financial markets rallied during 1985–86. However, the Louvre Accord proved more elusive when US officials criticized their counterparts in Germany and Japan for raising interest rates. This policy dispute contributed to the stock market crash of October 1987. While many observers at the time believed the stock market sell-off would trigger a US recession, it proved to be a "false alarm," as the economy and markets recovered in 2008 after the Fed and other central banks eased monetary policies.

Portfolio Positioning

The optimal investment strategy during the Plaza Accord was to be long US financial assets, but to be underweight the dollar. Japanese investors, however, failed to grasp the importance of hedging their currency exposure to US bonds, and they ultimately lost money on their positions. Thereafter, investors needed to pare back positions in US financial assets when the USA was entering the crisis zone in 1987. Over the longer term, the optimal strategy in an environment of steady disinflation was to be long financial assets and underweight commodities.

Notes

1. This equation can be derived from two accounting identities, in which GDP is defined as the sum of C+I+G+X–M and also the sum of C+S+T.

2. See Nicholas Sargen, "International Capital Flows: Framework, Directions and Investment Implications." Salomon Brothers Bond Market Research, April 1990.
3. For an excellent discussion of the events surrounding the Louvre Accord see Solomon, *The Confidence Game*, Chaps. 18–19.
4. Ibid., p. 337.
5. Ibid., p. 351.
6. Ibid., p. 393.

6

Speculators Attack the Concept of European Monetary Union

The early 1990s marked a period of new-found optimism about the prospects for Europe, following disappointing economic performance on the continent during much of the 1980s. The key development was the 1992 project that would transform the European Community (EC) from a customs union arrangement into a fully integrated market in which "the free movement of goods, persons, services and capital is ensured."[1] From a European perspective, the prospect of an integrated market that would surpass the US economy in size proved exciting to businesses and governments alike, and it contributed to an investment boom in Europe.

For many Americans, however, the 1992 project was an enigma. Some believed the single market would make it more difficult for US businesses to compete inside Europe. Others were skeptical that European countries could put aside national interests and reconcile their differences to achieve the long-standing goal of European integration.

The immediacy of the situation became apparent when the Berlin Wall collapsed in late 1989, and the West German government sought rapid unification for East and West Germany. Suddenly, financial markets were pressed to supply capital to finance the reconstruction of Eastern Europe, and interest rates in Europe surged above those in the USA for the first time in more than a decade. This had important ramifications for the USA and other countries that had to compete more intensively for international capital. Many investors wondered if this meant that the USA would now be more influenced by developments in Europe than in the past.

Investors also had to assess the agreement reached by EC members at Maastricht in late 1991 to achieve Economic and Monetary Union (EMU) by

© The Editor(s) (if applicable) and The Author(s) 2016
N.P. Sargen, *Global Shocks*, DOI 10.1007/978-3-319-41105-7_6

January 1, 1999. How committed were each of the 12 members to meet the criteria to become part of a single currency? And which countries were likely to gain the most from economic and monetary union—the leading members such as Germany and France, or the periphery, including the UK, Italy, Spain, Portugal and Ireland? During 1992–93 a speculative attack by prominent hedge funds nearly aborted the launch of the EMU, and it was a precursor of the turmoil in the eurozone that surfaced in 2010–12.

Europe Enjoys an Investment Boom

Prior to the sweeping changes in Eastern Europe in 1989, Western Europe was enjoying its strongest economic growth in more than a decade (see Table 6.1). The economic upswing that began in 1983 gathered strength in the late 1980s, as business fixed investment accelerated in the four largest economies (West Germany, France, Italy and the UK) to about 10 % annualized.

This represented the fastest rate of capital formation over any sustained period since the late 1960s.[2]

The investment boom was a product of both cyclical and structural developments. On the cyclical side, the four major economies experienced a significant increase in corporate profits as a share of gross domestic product (GDP) in the late 1980s. In most instances, this reversed a plunge in profits that occurred in the 1970s, when oil prices spiked. At the same time, businesses began to face capacity constraints as domestic demand accelerated.

The most important structural development was the government-sponsored project to begin the formation of a single European market in 1992. While the goal of creating a single European market dates back to the 1950s, it was not until the mid to late 1980s that European officials became fully engaged in making it a reality. During early 1986, the EC member states ratified the

Table 6.1 Real gross national product (GNP) growth (in %)

	1979–87	1988	1989	1990
Europe	2.1	3.7	3.4	2.7
Germany	1.7	3.6	4.0	3.3
France	1.9	3.7	3.6	3.1
Italy	2.5	3.9	3.4	3.0
UK	2.2	4.3	2.4	1.1
Spain	2.4	5.0	4.9	4.1
Japan	4.5	5.7	5.0	4.5
USA	2.7	4.4	2.9	1.5

Source: JPMorgan, World Financial Markets, February 1990

Single European Act that committed them to the establishment of an internal market by the end of 1992. However, the groundswell for the project did not take hold for another two years. In mid-1989, *The Economist's* survey of Europe's internal market began with the following observation:

> Little more than a year ago, Europeans themselves barely realized that the 12 European Community countries had found a real resolve to turn themselves into one open market by the end of 1992. It was only after the wrangle over the EEC's budget and farm policies had been settled in February 1988 that their governments woke up to the task they had set themselves more than two years earlier. The pace of construction picked up in 1988, helped by the weight and competence of West Germany as president of the European Council during the first half of the year. But the significance of this project for the rest of the world still rated barely a passing thought among its architects.[3]

For many European businesses the prospect of a pan-European market meant that they could expand and rationalize operations, while reaping greater economies of scale (see Table 6.2). Consequently, firms within the EC that previously limited their operations to their home market now sought to build sales and market share across the community. At the same time, non-European firms sought to establish operations within the EC to avoid possible exclusion from the market.

In an article on the 1992 initiative, Professor David R. Cameron notes:

> There can be no doubt that one of the main beneficiaries of the internal market initiative will be European business. The initiative offers European producers of goods and services the prospect of competing in a market of more than 300 mil-

Table 6.2 Exports of EC members to other EC (% of exports)

	1960	1972	1985
West Germany	29.5	39.9	47.4
France	29.8	48.8	47.6
Italy	29.6	45.0	46.1
Netherlands	45.9	64.8	72.5
Belgium–Lux.	50.3	68.3	69.1
UK	15.2	22.5	46.1
Ireland	6.5	15.6	6.8
Denmark	27.5	22.1	43.4
Greece	32.9	48.7	53.1
Spain	38.5	35.4	49.9
Portugal	21.5	20.2	58.4

Source: IMF, Direction of Trade, *Euro-Politics*, Alberta M. Sbragia, editor

lion people. Moreover, they will have a privileged position in relation to non-European producers. The reduction or elimination of national barriers to trade and commerce – whether in the form of frontier formalities, technical standards in public procurement, or company law – offers European firms an opportunity to reduce transactions costs, achieve economies of scale, and thereby improve profitability. The liberalizing and deregulatory thrust of the 1992 initiative encourages firms to obtain those scale economies rapidly, through cross-national alliances and joint ventures.[4]

Interest Rates Surge

The strengthening of the European economies and business investment, in turn, created significant upward pressure on European interest rates, especially as inflation in the region accelerated. Inflation in West Germany, for example, nearly doubled to 3 % in 1989 from 1.8 % the previous year. Meanwhile, inflation in Italy and the UK jumped a percentage point each to 6.5 % and 7.7 %, respectively. By comparison, inflation in the USA was little changed at 4.5 %.

To contain these pressures and also to counter the weakness of the deutsche mark versus the dollar, the Bundesbank tightened monetary policy repeatedly in 1989. Most other European central banks followed suit, as they sought to keep their currencies in a narrow band against the deutsche mark. These actions helped to strengthen the deutsche mark and other European currencies against the dollar. But they did not calm nervous bondholders, especially when the Berlin Wall came down in early November. It triggered a chain reaction throughout Eastern Europe in which old-line communist rulers were toppled one by one and were replaced by pro-western leaders.

Businesspeople, investors and policymakers alike subsequently began to consider the prospect for reconstruction of the Eastern bloc countries, whose population of 110 million was roughly one-third of the EC. Few observers at the time doubted that the reconstruction of the former Soviet bloc countries would require extensive financing from both public and private sources. But there was considerable uncertainty about the magnitude of financing required and how easily it could be absorbed in world capital markets.

Market attention was concentrated on the ballooning public sector borrowing requirement for the unified German government. It soared to about 4.7 % of GDP in 1990 from virtual balance for the West German government in 1989. And the unified deficit was projected to rise to 5 % of GDP in 1991.[5] In response, long-term bond yields in West Germany surged by two percentage points to 9 %.

A Global Capital Shortage?

As the 1990s began, investors worried about a worldwide capital shortage. The surge in European interest rates at the beginning of the decade boosted them above those in the USA for the first time in more than a decade.[6] And Europe, which previously had been an exporter of capital to the rest of the world, was now importing capital from abroad to help finance the 1992 project and reconstruction of Eastern Europe.

At the same time, the Bank of Japan under newly appointed Governor Mieno tightened monetary policy significantly to counter "asset price" inflation in that country. The restraint was also intended to prevent the Japanese economy from overheating, as capital spending failed to respond quickly to higher interest rates and a falling stock market. Indeed, real Japanese investment in plant and equipment soared to a record 25 % or real GNP in 1990 and approached $650 billion—surpassing investment spending in the USA.[7] This policy shift resulted in a significant narrowing of interest rate differentials between the USA and Japan, and led to an abrupt slowing in Japanese capital outflows.

Meanwhile, the US economy and financial system were feeling the impact of high real interest rates. Problems with saving and loan associations that surfaced in the late 1980s continued to mount, and in February 1990 the junk-bond market seized up, when Drexel Burnham Lambert failed. Conditions in the commercial banking sector also deteriorated in the spring, when the Bank of New England fell into crisis, requiring support from the Treasury and Federal Reserve.

Normally, the Federal Reserve would have eased monetary policy in these circumstances. However, the Fed was inhibited in doing so when central banks in Europe and Japan were tightening policies, and the USA confronted diminished capital inflows from abroad and pressures on the dollar. And with real interest rates in Europe and Japan well above those in the USA, many observers were concerned that US bond yields would stay relatively high, even during a period of US economic weakness.

German Monetary Unification

The situation became even more complicated in the summer of 1990, when Chancellor Kohl of West Germany made rapid unification his number one priority. To encourage East Germany to approve unification, Kohl agreed to allow East German ostmarks to be converted into deutsche marks at a 1:1 rate. Kohl also endorsed the concept of wage parity between East and West Germany, even though labor productivity in the East was considerably lower than in the West. These actions were widely criticized at the time for being unrealistic and for creating problems for economic integration of the two countries. As Steven Solomon observed:

> The Kohl Government's dash to GMU confiscated wealth from West Germany and gave it to East Germans, who went on a short-lived spending spree. But their 35 percent wage increase far outstripped their productivity gains. East German firms soon collapsed…
>
> Kohl's insistence on extending government welfare parity to the East and his rejection of tax increases or spending cuts to pay for it undid a decade of budgetary consolidation. A 1989 fiscal surplus turned into a deficit of over 5.5 percent of GDP in 1991. Government borrowing exploded. The one-to-one conversion rate led to a 15 percent increase in total German money supply.[8]

These actions disturbed Bundesbank President Pohl, who believed that rapid monetary union was a mistake. Accordingly, the Bundesbank responded by tightening monetary policy in Volcker-like fashion. Short-term interest rates leapt above long rates, producing the steepest yield curve inversion in German history.

Amid these developments, world financial markets were jolted by yet another surprise, when Iraq invaded Kuwait in early August. The disruption in Kuwaiti oil supplies caused oil prices to spike to nearly $40 per barrel, and it triggered a worldwide sell-off of stocks and bonds. The US economy slipped into recession, as households and businesses stopped spending whilst waiting to see how the US and international community would respond to the Iraqi action.

Steps Toward Monetary Union

It was against this backdrop that the European Council met in Maastricht in December 1991 to lay the groundwork for the EMU. The goal was to transform the existing European Monetary System (EMS) into a full-fledged monetary union, in which there was a single currency and a European Central Bank (ECB), by January 1, 1999.

This represented a landmark development. When the EMS was conceived by the leaders of France and Germany in the late 1970s, the idea was to create a "zone of monetary stability." In light of the extraordinary currency volatility then, a fixed exchange rate regime within Europe was deemed impractical. By the mid-1980s, however, the EMS had evolved into a quasi-fixed exchange rate regime.

The key turning point for the EMS occurred in 1983, when the French government under Francois Mitterrand abandoned its highly expansionary policies to bring them more in line with Germany's. Over time, other European countries followed the French example of pursuing more orthodox policies, and subsequent EMS currency realignments after 1983 generally involved more modest adjustments in parities. As David Cameron observes:

> The 1983 realignment – precipitated by continued downward pressure on the French franc in response to continued trade deficits, budget deficits, and high inflation rates – demonstrated that countries could not reflate against the tide of German price stability. If they did, they would eventually find themselves in the position of the French Socialists in 1983. That is, they would have to either sacrifice demand stimulation for austerity and price stability or leave the EMS.[9]

By the late 1980s, an increasing number of European countries pursued policies to bring their inflation rates in line with Germany's (see Table 6.3). This, in turn, resulted in a convergence of interest rates within Europe, and only modest adjustments of parities within the EMS. Most of the EMS member countries were able to maintain narrow bands for their currencies of 2 ¼ % around their central parities, while the Spanish peseta and British pound were included in the EMS with 6 % bands.

At Maastricht, the European Council formalized a set of criteria that countries needed to meet to become part of a common European currency. They included:[10]

Table 6.3 CPI inflation in the EC (%)

	1980	1985	1988
Currency in EMS			
West Germany	5.5	2.2	1.2
Netherlands	6.5	2.2	0.7
Belgium	6.6	4.9	1.2
Luxembourg	6.3	4.1	1.4
France	13.3	5.8	2.7
Italy	21.2	9.2	5.0
Denmark	12.3	4.7	4.6
Ireland	18.2	5.4	2.1
Currency not in EMS			
UK	18.0	6.1	4.9
Spain	15.6	8.8	4.8
Portugal	16.6	19.6	9.7
Greece	24.9	19.3	13.5

Source: *Euro-Politics*, Alberta M. Sbragia, editor, p. 48

- Price stability, defined as a rate of inflation within 1.5 percentage points of the three best-performing EU countries.
- Low long-term interest rates, defined as within two percentage points of the three lowest-scoring EU countries.
- Exchange rate stability, meaning that for at least two years the respective country kept its currency within the normal fluctuation margins of Europe's exchange rate mechanism (ERM).
- A sustainable government financial position, defined as a budget deficit no higher than 3 % of GDP, and a ratio of public debt to GDP no higher than 60 %.

A timetable was also established for the EMS members to ratify the Maastricht Treaty, either through a vote of their legislatures or the populace at large.

Market Response to Maastricht

Financial markets responded favorably to the concept of EMU, and global fixed-income investors sought to benefit from it through so-called convergence trades. As inflation rates in Europe converged toward Germany's, portfolio managers typically would overweight higher-yielding bond markets such as Spain, Portugal, Italy and the UK and underweight lower-yielding markets such as Germany and Holland. They would also hedge their currency exposure into dollars by selling lower-yielding currencies. They did so to lower their hedging costs; otherwise, the returns would have been comparable to US dollar instruments.

This strategy proved highly successful in the late 1980s and early 1990s, because the higher-yielding currencies were able to maintain their parities against the deutsche mark. Investors took comfort that currency realignments within the EMS were small and had become less frequent. While the strategy could backfire if there was a broad-based realignment, many investors believed this risk had diminished.

Market conditions shifted markedly in May 1992, however, when Danish voters—by the narrowest of margins—failed to ratify the Maastricht Treaty. This event heightened tensions within the EMS, as market participants began to worry about public support for the EMU. The French referendum on Maastricht that was scheduled for mid-September was considered a litmus test for the treaty, and indications were that the vote would be very close. Many macro hedge funds responded by shorting the high-yielding currencies, while global fixed-income managers lessened their exposure to the higher-yielding markets and switched funds into the core markets.

Tensions in the EMS heightened in July, when the Bundesbank increased the discount rate by 75 basis points to 8.75 %, which put pressure on other member central banks to match. The breaking point was reached in early September, when the Italian lira was forced outside the narrow exchange rate bands. Soon after, the British pound came under attack. The Bundesbank responded by lowering short-term interest rates, and the UK authorities borrowed in the capital markets, adding foreign exchange reserves to mount a defense, while also raising interest rates. However, the attempt to defend sterling proved fruitless when it was reported that Bundesbank's President Schlesinger was skeptical that the existing parity could be maintained. This incident triggered an imminent devaluation of the pound that forced sterling outside the ERM, along with the Italian lira and Spanish peseta, and it reportedly reaped a profit of over 1 billion dollars for George Soros.

The attack on the ERM subsequently spread to the French franc. The French authorities were able to defend the parity for the franc when the French electorate—by the narrowest of margins—ratified the Maastricht Treaty. However, pressures on the franc resurfaced in mid-1993, when currency speculators sensed that the French government's resolve to keep interest rates high was waning, as French unemployment soared past 3 million. The French government responded by intervening massively to support the franc, along with the German authorities, and it subsequently widened the band for the franc to 15 % from 2¼ %, so as not to give currency speculators an easy target. These actions ultimately proved to be sufficient to convince investors that French–German cooperation, which was the core of the eurozone concept, was solid—and speculative pressures subsided over time.

The attack on the ERM occurred while I served as chief investment officer for Prudential Insurance's global bond and currency unit. It was the first time in my career that I had direct responsibility for managing money, which is very different from being a strategist who advises people on how to position portfolios. I quickly learned that while the quadrant framework worked very well during my stint at Salomon Brothers, positioning investment portfolios became very tricky when markets fluctuated between being in "risk on" mode and "risk off" mode.

Throughout this period I believed that the eurozone concept would not be derailed by the attack on it by hedge funds.[11] Nonetheless, I adopted a neutral stance in summer 1992, because I did not understand what was happening in the markets. I subsequently reinstated positions during 1993 when I became convinced that markets had overreacted. Staying flexible ultimately proved to be the correct strategy, as many mutual fund managers who maintained over-weight positions in higher-yielding currencies and bonds were forced to exit the business during the sell-off period. In addition to focusing on economic fundamentals, I also learned that a savvy investor needed to be aware how other prominent managers were positioning their portfolios, as their actions could affect markets for extended periods.

Perspective on the Launch of the EMU

The decision by the EC to establish a monetary union with a single currency and a European Central Bank ranks among the most important developments in the post-war era. Investors at the time had to decide whether this objective was attainable. The concept was tested when Denmark failed to ratify the Maastricht Treaty, which led prominent hedge fund managers to conclude that the periphery countries such as the UK, Italy, Spain, Portugal and Ireland would not be able to meet the criteria.

Looking back on the 1992–93 crisis, what stands out today is how fixated the policymakers and investors were on achieving convergence of inflation and interest rates as a necessary condition for the launch of the eurozone, while many longer-term considerations were left for academic economists to ponder. The concept of monetary union was strongly endorsed by European leaders for political reasons, even though many economists at the time were skeptical that Europe constituted an "optimum currency area." Indeed, the skeptics believed that the member countries eventually would discover that the benefits of monetary union were outweighed by the costs.

One disadvantage cited then was limited European labor mobility. It meant that if there was an adverse shock in one part of Europe, the unemployed would be reluctant to migrate to another part, given the diversity of languages and cultures. A second disadvantage was the lack of a European fiscal union to complement monetary union. This meant there was no mechanism for making transfer payments from a central government to the various national govern-ments in Europe. Consequently, countries that experienced high unemploy-ment faced the burden of adjusting by cutting real wages significantly, because the existence of monetary union precluded the members from depreciating their currencies or pursuing independent monetary policies.

These issues did not concern investors when monetary union was being contemplated, primarily because Europe was enjoying strong economic growth in the 1990s, and once France and Germany demonstrated resolve to maintain the DM–franc parity, the stage was set for the launch of the euro in

1999. During the ensuing decade, inflation differentials in the eurozone continued to narrow, and spreads in bond yields within the eurozone compressed to all-time lows.

The initial assessment was that the euro had been launched successfully, and the winners were the periphery countries that benefitted from falling interest rates, capital inflows and strong economic growth. In a publication commemorating the tenth anniversary of the European Central Bank, the experiment with the creation of the euro was acclaimed albeit with several important caveats:

> These ten years have shown the foundations of EMU were sound and that a high degree of economic convergence had been achieved by those countries that adopted the euro. However, several challenges remain. Most euro area countries still need to enhance their flexibility and adaptability to shocks. In other words, they must continue structural reform of their product and labor markets... National governments must also continuously monitor developments in national competitiveness. Financial integration has made great strides, but further progress is necessary in several segments (such as cross border banking). The EU's framework has not yet reached a steady state.[12]

The caveats acknowledged in this report proved to be prescient two years later, when the newly elected Greek government announced that the country's budget deficit and debt outstanding were considerably larger than had been reported previously. Once investors gained wind of this, they became concerned about sovereign credit risk, especially for countries with sizeable budget deficits and debt outstanding such as Greece, Ireland, Italy, Portugal and Spain. Over the next two years, their bond yields surged mainly reflecting a marked widening in credit spreads versus German bunds. As these countries fell into severe recession and unemployment climbed to record levels, they had to undertake austerity programs to bring their debt down to more sustainable levels. Investors, in turn, were left to wonder how long the electorate would endure the hardships, and whether some countries would opt out of the eurozone or be forced out.

From this experience, it became clear that the design of the eurozone left it vulnerable during periods of economic weakness. One problem was that there was no central oversight of Europe's financial system, and the various national regulators applied different standards to oversee banks in their respective countries. Even more surprising was the lack of a true lender of last resort to provide liquidity during times of financial stress. Then, just when it appeared that the very existence of the eurozone was being called into question in mid-

2012, Mario Draghi, the head of the ECB, announced that it was prepared to do "whatever it takes" to preserve the viability of the euro. Investors interpreted this statement to mean that the ECB was prepared to buy bonds of its members and to provide necessary financing to avoid a collapse of the financial system. This proved sufficient to restore investor confidence in the eurozone and over the next two years bond yields declined and credit spreads narrowed back to pre-crisis levels.

This action did not dispel worries completely, however, as the eurozone confronted a new crisis in the first half of 2015, when the newly elected Greek government rejected the measures that the creditors mandated for it to receive a third bailout program. This situation nearly resulted in Greece being expelled from the eurozone, but the Greek government ultimately acquiesced and was allowed to remain a member. Nonetheless, the situation is precarious, with Greece having experienced its worst depression in the post-war era and the country's banking system in tatters.

Long-Term Prospects for the Eurozone

Amid all that has happened, the question most investors ask today is "Where is the eurozone headed?"

My answer is that the long-term prospects for it remain clouded if policymakers are unable to restore economic growth and lower unemployment. While the current governments in the eurozone are committed to the euro and monetary union for political reasons, the risk is that the electorate of one or more member countries could become disenchanted and elect leaders who are opposed to ongoing austerity, such as occurred in Greece.

My former colleague and current professor at New York University, Kim Schoenholtz, sums it up very well in a commentary entitled "The Importance of Being Europe."[13] He contends that despite its name, the EMU was not and is not primarily an economic endeavor. Instead, the founders viewed the EMU as a profound step toward a more perfect political union:

> Their experience with the disaster of 20th century European nationalism led them to expect that these stresses would cause European leaders to make greater sacrifices of sovereignty to save and advance political union.
>
> That outcome remains possible, but it was never preordained… While Europeans generally support the euro, *"they generally show no appetite to delegate more power to the European Union."*… Instead, the persistent economic stresses

in the member states… are nurturing the strongest anti-European political reactions since efforts to promote integration began in the 1950s.

In this respect, the long-standing debate about whether Europe is an optimum currency area is far from resolved. Accordingly, investors today must be cognizant of sovereign credit risks in the eurozone, and the possibility that one or more members could exit it.

Conclusions

The creation of the EMU ranks among the most important developments in the post-war era. While European politicians viewed it as a means to ensure stability in Europe and to prosper economically, financial markets have tested the resolve of policymakers to meet the mandated criteria on several occasions.

Diagnosis of Problem
Following the adoption of the Maastricht Treaty in 1991, the central issue was whether countries in the European periphery would meet the criteria for becoming members of the eurozone. The challenge for these countries became greater in the aftermath of German unification, when the Bundesbank tightened monetary policy substantially in order to counter rising inflation.

Policy Response
Most countries in the periphery pursued the prescribed course of tightening monetary policies in order to keep their currencies within the requisite bands, while also bringing their inflation rates in line with Germany's.

Market Response
Investors initially backed the eurozone concept by purchasing higher-yielding bonds in the periphery while selling lower-yielding currencies (mainly DM and Swiss franc) versus the dollar. Following Denmark's rejection of the Maastricht Treaty, however, several prominent hedge funds placed massive bets that countries on the periphery would not be able to keep their currencies in the prescribed bands. The most notable incident occurred when British sterling was forced outside its band in September 1992.

Portfolio Positioning
The main challenge in positioning investment portfolios during the initial test of the EMU in 1992–93 was that markets fluctuated between being in

"risk on" mode (the bliss zone) and "risk off" mode (the crisis zone). This made managing money extremely challenging. During this period I learned the importance of being flexible when I did not fully understand what was happening in the markets. Therefore, I concluded it was prudent to pare back risks during the sell-off phase and to wait until I was more confident before re-establishing risky positions. This experience also helped me to navigate through the treacherous markets of 2010–12, when the same pattern of market behavior was evident.

Notes

1. See David R. Cameron, "The 1992 Initiative; Causes and Consequences" in *Euro-Politics,* Brookings Institution, Washington, DC, December 1991.
2. JP Morgan, *World Financial Markets*, "The Decade of Europe?" February 14, 1990.
3. *The Economist*, "A Survey of Europe's Internal Market", July 8, 1989.
4. Cameron, "The 1992 Initiative", pp. 48–49.
5. Solomon, *The Confidence Game*, p. 473.
6. Note: In the early 1980s, by comparison, U.S. short-term interest rates were as much as 10 % points higher than those in Germany.
7. Solomon, *The Confidence Game*, pp. 473–4.
8. Ibid., pp. 46–47.
9. Cameron, "The 1992 Initiative", p. 47.
10. *The Economist*, "A Survey of Europe's Internal Market".
11. Note: One of the main considerations influencing me was a speech by Chancellor Kohl in New York in which he explained that the EMU was vital to lesson worries about German unification. My assessment was that political imperative would supersede economic considerations at that time.
12. European Central Bank, *Monthly Bulletin*, 10th Anniversary of the ECB, July 2008.
13. October 27, 2014 commentary by Kermit Schoenholtz.

Part II

Easy Credit Breeds Asset Bubbles and Instability

7

Japan's Bubble Culminates in Two Decades of Deflation

Throughout much of the post-World War II era, Japan was the world's most dynamic economy. Its economic growth rate far surpassed that of the USA and Europe, and it emerged in the 1980s as the world's largest capital exporter on the back of a powerful export machine that generated persistent large trade and current account surpluses. In 1985 the economy was hit by a "yen shock" as the leading industrial economies drafted the Plaza Accord to produce an orderly decline of the dollar. Yet Japan appeared extremely resilient: The economy grew by 4–5 % per annum in the second half of the 1980s, while the stock market and real estate values soared as interest rates fell to record lows.

Conditions changed dramatically by the end of the decade, however, when the Bank of Japan tightened monetary policy to combat "asset price" inflation. While Japan's economy withstood the initial tightening, it stagnated in the early 1990s, as the stock market and real estate market both dropped precipitously. Over the next two decades the economy was mired in a low growth trap that over time created deflationary pressures.

This dramatic about-face in economic performance poses several questions for investors:

1. What went so wrong to transform a dynamic economy into one that languished for two decades?
2. What lessons does Japan's experience hold for the USA and other countries?
3. How could investors have lost sight of reality in driving Japanese stocks and real estate to such unsustainable levels?

© The Editor(s) (if applicable) and The Author(s) 2016
N.P. Sargen, *Global Shocks*, DOI 10.1007/978-3-319-41105-7_7

Japan's Economic Miracle

Following the devastation of World War II, the Japanese economy experienced unprecedented economic growth that averaged more than 10 % per annum in the 1960s, and which far surpassed that of the USA and Europe in the 1970s and 1980s. While some of the outperformance was the result of Japan being able to rebuild and play catch-up after the war, its high growth rate was also supported by high rates of saving and investment and a development strategy based on strong export growth. Japan's economic performance, however, was far from uniform. The largest corporations were geared to produce for overseas markets including the USA and Europe, while many smaller businesses that were family owned provided services for the domestic economy that lagged behind those in other industrial countries.

The transformation of Japan from a war-ravished economy to a global superpower occurred over several phases under the direction of one of the most powerful agencies of the Japanese government, the Ministry of International Trade and Industry (MITI). The first stage in the 1950s stressed increased coal and steel production and developing heavy industries such as shipbuilding and timber production. During the second phase in the 1960s and 1970s the focus shifted to producing consumer products and automobiles for the export market. The third phase, which went into high gear in the 1980s, saw the development of knowledge-based products such as computers and consumer electronics.

Throughout this period, Japanese economic policy was generally viewed in a favorable light internationally. To outsiders the close alliance between government and business was a powerful combination that earned the nickname "Japan Inc." The Japanese government was also credited with pursuing macroeconomic policies that limited budgetary imbalances and kept inflation under control. The Japanese people also were highly educated and adaptable. In 1979, an eminent scholar, Professor Ezra Vogel of Harvard, wrote a book *Japan as Number One*, which proclaimed, "Japan has dealt more successfully with more of the basic problems of post-industrial society than any other country."[1]

This optimism, in part, reflected the tremendous resilience of the Japanese economy and people. During the mid-1970s, the country was caught off guard by the first oil shock, but it subsequently adopted policies to conserve on energy and to lessen its vulnerability to future oil shocks. Thus, when the second oil shock occurred in 1979 and the early 1980s, the economy was better equipped to deal with the impact of surging oil prices. By the mid-1980s, when oil prices fell precipitously, Japan amassed record trade and current account surpluses, and its holdings of overseas assets rivaled those of the Organization of the Petroleum Exporting Companies (OPEC) during the 1970s. At the same time, the USA ran record external deficits that were financed in large part by Japanese purchases of US bonds both by the Bank of Japan and institutional investors such as life insurance companies and trust banks.

Endaka (High Yen) Period

The large bilateral trade imbalances spawned increasing trade tensions between the USA and Japan, in which US officials criticized Japan for manipulating the yen. In September 1985, the five leading industrial countries; USA, Japan, West Germany, United Kingdom and France reached the Plaza Accord that was designed to produce an orderly decline in the value of the dollar. Over the remainder of the decade the yen appreciated by about 50 % against the dollar, while Japanese inflation stayed below that in the USA (see Fig. 7.1). The yen's real appreciation surpassed that of the US dollar and the British pound in the first half of the decade, and both countries eventually had to ease monetary policies to restore international price competitiveness.

Similarly, the surge in the yen raised concerns among Japanese policymakers about the impact it would have on export growth and overall economic growth. Amid evidence that the Japanese economy was slowing markedly,

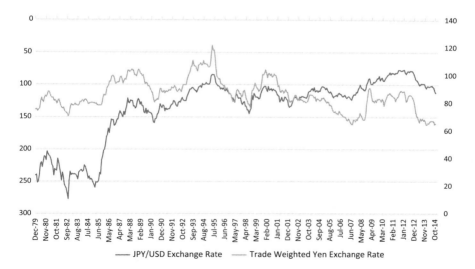

Fig. 7.1 Yen/US exchange and trade-weighted yen exchange rate (Source: JP Morgan)

from 5 % in 1985 to 2.5 % in 1986, the Bank of Japan eased monetary policy aggressively, lowering the official discount rate from 5 % to 2.5 %. This ushered in a period of low interest rates and rapid growth of money and credit that lasted until the end of the decade. The economy once again proved resilient, as real gross domestic product (GDP) growth rebounded to 4 % in 1987 and 6 % in 1988.

These developments, in turn, caused Japanese businesses and financial institutions to adapt their behavior. Japanese multinationals responded by increasingly shifting the locus of production offshore, especially to emerging Asia, where production costs were significantly lower than in Japan. At the same time, companies embarked on programs to lower costs by investing in plant and equipment while financing the expansion primarily through debt issuance. From 1986 until 1990, Japanese companies increased capital invest-ment by 11 % annually, and the country's capital stock expanded by more than 40 % cumulatively, twice the increase in the USA.

The ability to obtain ready financing on easy terms also gave rise to wide-spread speculation and so-called "*zaitech*" finance. As export-dependent industries such as shipbuilding, steel and autos faced a severe profit squeeze, other companies thrived as they borrowed funds on very easy terms, including convertible debt issuance, and created entities that reinvested the proceeds in the Japanese stock market. These investment vehicles added to the companies' reported profitability as the Japanese stock market soared. (Some observers at the time estimated that as much as 40–50 % of total reported profits from Japan's largest corporations were derived from "*zaitech*.")

The potential for an asset bubble was also affected by the unique nature of Japanese bank regulation, which allowed Japanese banks to count stock mar-ket holdings as "primary capital."[2] (Such practice is not permitted by US or European bank regulation.) This practice is very pro-cyclical, as it risks bank capital being wiped out if there is a sharp contraction in stock (or real estate) values. The situation was compounded by Japanese bank lending practices in which banks accepted property as collateral for loans, and land in effect served as an engine for credit expansion.

As long as monetary policy stayed easy, it appeared that Japanese companies had found a way to overcome the impact of the strong yen. Many companies reported strong earnings on the back of speculative investment activity, while financial institutions and households benefitted from soaring values of equi-ties and land prices. However, the underlying business and financial structures supporting the economy were becoming increasingly risky.[3]

Monetary Tightening Bursts the Bubble

The bubble burst at the end of the decade when the newly appointed Governor of the Bank of Japan, Yashui Mieno, began tightening monetary policy in order to combat "asset price inflation." Japan's discount rate was boosted from 2.5 % in 1989 to 6 % in 1990 (See Fig. 7.2). At the same time, the Bank of Japan ordered the commercial banks to reduce their total lending by 30 % and jaw-boned them to cease lending to real estate firms and property speculators. All told, these actions caused money supply growth (M2+CD) to plummet from 12 % in 1988 to zero by 1992. (See Fig. 7.3).

The impact on the stock market was immediate, as the Nikkei 225 average plummeted by more than 50 % from the end of 1989 until 1992 (see Fig. 7.4). Values for land prices also declined, although the magnitude was difficult to capture due to the relatively small volume of transactions.[4]

Despite these developments, the overall economy held up surprisingly well: Real GDP continued to grow at 4 %+ until 1992, and Japan's trade surplus continued to mount. Some of the resiliency was due to Japan's practice of lifetime employment, as companies kept redundant labor on the payrolls even though profits sagged. Furthermore, businesses continued to add to capacity even though there was considerable excess capacity. Japanese households also drew down savings to maintain their lifestyles.

By 1992–93, however, economic growth came to a grinding halt, and the economy slipped into recession. Total employment contracted for the first

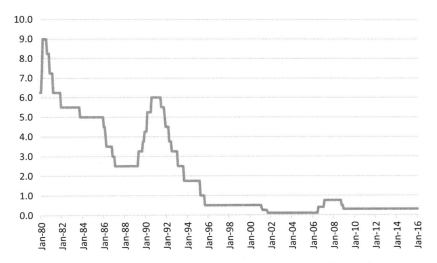

Fig. 7.2 Bank of Japan discount rate (in %) (Source: Bank of Japan)

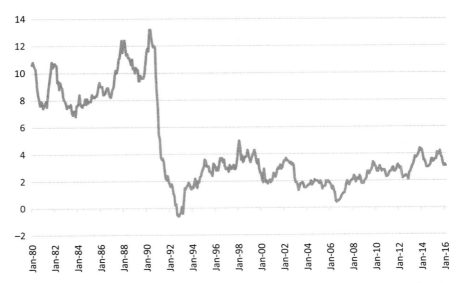

Fig. 7.3 Japanese money supply growth (M2), year to year % change (Source: Bank of Japan)

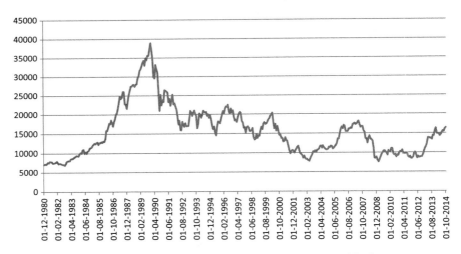

Fig. 7.4 Japanese stock market: Nikkei 225 Index (Source: Nikkei)

time in seven years, and company profits shrank for a third consecutive year for the first time in the post-war era. The mood of the country shifted markedly, as the self-assurance about the success of Japanese-style capitalism gave way to fear that Japan had lost its way.

With signs of panic ensuing, Japan's Ministry of Finance tried to halt the slide in the stock market by investing money held in public pensions and postal savings directly in the stock market. Nonetheless, the so-called "price-keeping operations" had only a temporary effect in bolstering the stock market.

Thereafter, the government placed increased pressure on the Bank of Japan to ease its grip on monetary policy, and by 1993 the discount rate was set at a record low of 1.75 %. This was accompanied by a series of government spending packages that were estimated to total 6 % of GDP. However, these programs had little impact on the economy as businesses were reluctant to boost investment spending, given the considerable excess capacity in the economy.

Deflation Sets In

By the middle of the 1990s, Japan's economy was experiencing a modest recovery. However, deflationary pressures were also setting in as the yen continued to appreciate and reached a new record high against the dollar. Japan's import price index fell steadily as a result of the yen's appreciation and a surge in cheap Asian merchandise imports. These developments contributed to outright declines in consumer prices.

The deflationary pressures also stemmed from problems in the financial sector, as the volume of non-performing loans (NPL) worsened steadily.[5] By 1997, it was apparent that the NPL problem could make some major institutions insolvent. Around the end of the year one of the 13 main city banks announced its failure, and the following week one of the largest securities firms collapsed. The government tried to quell fears that Japan's financial system was close to a systemic collapse, by introducing legislation that enabled it to inject public funds into viable banks. However, banks were reluctant to ask for assistance, fearing they would be judged to be weak. The situation worsened in mid-1998, when Japan experienced the largest bank failure in history, which required the government to nationalize it.

The cumulative effect was to plunge Japan's economy back into recession. The policy response this time was more aggressive. A "zero interest rate policy" (ZIRP) was introduced in early 1999, and the government embarked on massive fiscal stimulus equivalent to 12 % of GDP during 1998–99. Legislation was also passed whereby an independent committee could effectively inject public funds without voluntary requests from troubled banks. The easing in monetary policy, however, was unable to overcome a tightening in credit conditions, as banks sought to restore their capital adequacy by shrinking their balance sheets.

The banks were reluctant to mark down their NPLs and erase their hidden reserves until they were required to do so by a newly created agency, the

Financial Services Agency (FSA).[6] It established a common standard to value NPLs and sent inspectors to the major banks to make sure they conformed to them. This process was critical in order to measure the amount of taxpayer money that was required to restore capital adequacy and to make shareholders assume the initial responsibility. The banking crisis did not end until 2003 when the Resona bank was nationalized and public funds equivalent to 9 % of GDP were injected to boost bank capital.

A Balance Sheet Recession

In looking back at Japan's experience it is clear the stagnation that set in after the bursting of the stock and real estate bubbles was very different from the typical business cycle that industrial countries experienced in the post-war era. Richard Koo, chief economist at Nomura Research Institute, was the first to label it a "balance-sheet recession" and to compare it with a typical "garden variety" recession.[7] The key difference is that the latter is mainly driven by inflation pressures, monetary policy tightening and inventory cycles, whereas a balance sheet recession is rooted in a mismatch between collapsing asset values and excessive debt liabilities that must be serviced. Koo argues that after the Japanese bubble burst, Japanese companies focused on minimizing their debt rather than maximizing profits. The net result was a surge in private sector saving that drove down incomes, prices and interest rates.

A balance sheet recession is also accompanied by a chronic lack of credit demand. Thus, as firms de-lever their balance sheets to reduce their debt burden, financial institutions are also under pressure to shrink their balance sheets to restore their capital adequacy. In these circumstances, Koo maintains that the government must step in to offset the decline in private sector spending. He contends that monetary policy becomes impotent as interest rates fall to zero and the authorities are unable to spur money and credit creation by injecting reserves into the banking system.

The latter view, however, was challenged by Benjamin Bernanke in 2002, when he served as vice chairman for the Federal Reserve. In a speech entitled, "Deflation: Making Sure 'It' Doesn't Happen Here,"[8] Bernanke disagreed with the premise that monetary policy was impotent:

> However, a principal message of my talk today is that a central bank whose accustomed policy rate has been forced down to zero has most definitely *not* run out of ammunition. A central bank, either alone or in cooperation with other

parts of the government, retains considerable power to expand aggregate demand and economic activity even when its accustomed policy rate is at zero.

In the body of his speech Bernanke foreshadowed policies including quantitative easing and "Operation Twist" that the Federal Reserve subsequently pursued after the 2008 financial crisis.

In the same speech Bernanke also offered his thoughts on why Japan was not able to end deflation. He cited two principal reasons. The first was that Japan faced significant barriers to growth, including massive financial problems in the banking and corporate sectors and a large overhang of government debt. He also acknowledged that private sector financial problems may have muted the effects of Japan's monetary policies. In this regard, he observed at the time, "Fortunately, the US does not share these problems."

The second consideration was that the failure to end deflation was a by-product of a long-standing political debate about how to address Japan's overall economic problems. Thus, while the Japanese realized the need for restoring both banks and corporations to solvency and for implementing structural changes to improve Japan's long-term economic health, politicians, economists, business people and the public at large had sharp differences about competing proposals for reform. He concluded his remarks with the following observation:

…in my view political constraints, rather than lack of policy instruments, explain why its deflation has persisted as long as it has. Thus, I do not view the Japanese experience as evidence against the general conclusion that US policymakers have the tools they need to prevent, and, if necessary, to cure a deflationary recession in the United States.

Differences from the US Experience

In light of what transpired six years later during the 2008 financial crisis, it is worthwhile to compare the Japanese and US experiences with asset bubbles. During the tech bubble in the second half of the 1990s, some observers contended that it would follow the same course as Japan, and a well-known chart was produced showing the similarities. These concerns resurfaced a decade later when the housing bubble burst.

Today, however, it is evident that the outcomes were considerably different in several respects. First, while the ensuing US and global recession in

2008–09 was far more severe than what Japan encountered in the 1990s, the US stock market recovered within a few years whereas the Japanese stock market remains about 50 % below its peak level 25 years later (see Fig. 7.5).

In my view the most important factor that accounts for this difference has to do with adjustments undertaken by the respective corporate sectors. In Japan's case, businesses did not respond to the deterioration in corporate profits by shedding labor or curbing capital spending; in fact, businesses continued to hire and increased plant and equipment several years after the bubble burst, which helped to prop up the economy initially. By comparison, US businesses adjusted rapidly to the financial crisis, shedding labor in droves and scaling back on capital spending. This response resulted in the economy falling into a deep recession, but it also led to a sharp V-shaped rebound in corporate profits that fueled the US stock market's recovery.

Second, despite the more severe downturn, the USA did not experience deflation, whereas Japan did from the mid-1990s through the following decade. As noted earlier, when the Bank of Japan (BOJ) burst Japan's asset bubble, it allowed money supply growth to fall to zero from 10–12 % growth in the late 1980s. Thereafter money supply growth fluctuated between 2–4 % for two decades. The BOJ did not ease its policy stance for two years despite the steep plunge in equity and real estate values, and it was not until late 1993

Fig. 7.5 The famous equity comparison (US versus Japanese market lagged 10 years)

that it brought the discount rate down below the level where it had begun to tighten policy in 1989.

In this regard, a critical difference is the swift and decisive monetary policy response under Federal Reserve Chairman Bernanke, which included the adoption of quantitative easing in which it expanded its balance sheet fourfold via purchases of treasuries and mortgage-backed securities. At the same time, US financial institutions were forced to write down the value of their assets due to mark-to-market accounting. This exacerbated the financial crisis during the 2007–09 time frame as mortgaged-backed securities and other structured vehicles plummeted in value. However, policy actions by the Federal Reserve to flood the market with liquidity, and the US government to inject capital into the banking system, stabilized the financial markets and laid the groundwork for the restoration of credit. In Japan, by comparison, banks continued to keep troubled loans on their books at par values, which were dubbed "zombie loans" that hindered new credit creation.

Finally, the strong rebound in the US stock market since early 2009 mirrored both a rapid recovery in corporate profits and the effects of low interest rates and quantitative easing. While many investors were skeptical that cost cutting in the US was sustainable, the surge in corporate profits initially stemmed from an expansion in profit margins and then broadened as top-line growth kicked in. For its part, there has been a close link between the size of the Fed's balance sheet and the broad market, as measured by the S&P 500 index, although the connection appears to be indirect rather than direct. In Japan, by comparison, the equity and real estate markets are still about half their values before the bubble burst.

Lessons for Investors and Policymakers

Japan's stock market and real estate bubble is important for investors and policymakers alike, because it represented the first incident of deflation in the post-war era. Japan's asset bubble poses a major challenge for a key tenet of efficient markets and modern portfolio theory (MPT) and the theory of efficient markets – namely, that investors are rational. This assumption clearly did not apply to Japanese investors, who drove valuations in the stock market to 80–90 times earnings, and real estate values to absurd levels, where the Emperor's Palace in Tokyo allegedly was worth more than all of the real estate in California.

This begs two questions. First, how could these valuations stray so far and so long from long-term equilibrium levels? Second, why did most economists and investors ignore what happened in Japan?

My answer to the first question is that in the wake of the success Japan enjoyed over several decades, investors became trend followers and could not conceive of developments that could alter the trend. Some observers justified the high-equity valuations on grounds that they stemmed from cross share-holdings of Japanese companies. Others took the growth of reported corporate profits at face value and discounted future flows at record low interest rates. With respect to real estate, high tax rates and land zoning restrictions hindered active trading, such that valuations often were based on hypothetical calculations. In the end, however, these explanations proved to be rationalizations for irrational behavior.

The second issue is harder to explain. My take is that western economists and investors viewed Japan as being unique and did not understand how businesses and financial institutions operated. Therefore, they were reluctant to draw broad conclusions based on Japan's experience. Thus, while Japanese multinationals were admired for their ability to compete globally, their corporate structure and governance was very different. Also, Japanese investors were not considered to be well trained in matters of finance and investing.

Over time, however, as the incidence of asset bubbles proliferated throughout the world to include the Asian financial crisis, the technology bubble and the 2008–09 financial crisis, the theory of efficient markets and MPT came under closer scrutiny. One of the lessons that investors should have learned from these experiences is that while policies of easy money and credit expansion often can fuel a boom over a long period, a subsequent tightening of these policies can unwind them very quickly.

The principal lesson for policymakers in this regard is the need to act quickly and decisively once a bubble has burst; otherwise there is likely to be a malevolent cycle of deleveraging by households, businesses and financial institutions as they attempt to reduce their debt burdens. Speed of response is essential in these circumstances, as the longer that policymakers delay countering deflation, the harder it becomes to circumvent it.

A Perspective on Japan's Bubble

Japan's bubble occurred while I was at Salomon Brothers Bond Market Research Department, where I headed fixed income research on the Asia/Pacific region. While I did not cover the Japanese stock market, I stayed on top of it by reading research produced by the Equity Research Department in Tokyo. The team in Tokyo was very bullish on the Japanese market, on the grounds that the economy was expanding at a healthy pace while inflation was tame, and they contended that the high price–earnings (P/E) multiples were justified by record low interest rates. This view, however, was directly at odds with reports by Bob Salomon, the head of Salomon's Equity Research Division, who contended that Japan's stock market was a bubble waiting to happen. (Note: The firm believed that researchers should express their own views, and that clients could make up their own minds about which one they believed. The kind interpretation is that the firm believed in free expression of research views; the less kind interpretation is it did not want to lose revenues derived from selling Japanese equities.)

At the time I was trying to assess whether the yen's 50 % real appreciation from 1985 to mid-1988 was sustainable. In June of that year I co-authored an article entitled "Japan's Adjustment Miracle and Its Implications for the Yen" with my colleague Kim Schoenholtz, an exceptional economist who covered the Japanese economy from Tokyo.[9] In the article Kim and I pointed out that while the yen's appreciation surpassed the dollar's surge under Ronald Reagan and sterling's under Margaret Thatcher, the key difference was that the yen's appreciation was accompanied by record low interest rates. By comparison, the strength of the UK sterling and the US dollar was associated with record high interest rates, and both currencies weakened considerably when monetary policy was eased.

Our report claimed that Japan had a better chance of adapting to a strong currency because of three factors: (1) a favorable shift in Japan's terms of trade (prices of exports relative to imports); (2) declining unit labor costs stemming from improved Japanese productivity combined with modest wage increases; and (3) overseas transfer of Japanese capital and technology to other parts of Asia. The report ended with the following conclusion: "**It appears that the yen will be the first currency in the floating exchange rate era to sustain a large, real appreciation**" (bolding included in report).

The conclusion about the yen turned out to be correct, but it was only after Japan's bubble burst that I realized the country in fact had been living on borrowed time. As the Japanese economy stagnated in the 1990s, it was increasingly evident that the yen had become too strong, and that this was an ongoing source of the deflationary pressures.

Nonetheless, to my surprise, the yen appreciated by more than 30 % against the dollar from 1992 until March 1995. The principal reason was that US officials were obsessed with Japan's large trade surplus with the USA, and US Treasury Secretary Lloyd Bentsen talked down the dollar on several occasions. This tactic made no sense to me, considering that the US economy was improving in 1993–94 while Japan was slipping into recession.

If I am critical of the Japanese policy response to deflation, I am equally critical of the role the US government played in exacerbating the situation by insisting on yen appreciation as a way to narrow Japan's current account surplus. The reason: The 70 % appreciation of the yen versus the dollar over ten years beginning in early 1985 had no discernible effect in reducing Japan's current account surplus! Fortunately, this misguided policy stance was abandoned when Robert Rubin became treasury secretary in 1995 and he adopted a strong dollar policy.

Finally, Japan's prolonged poor showing after the bubble burst fundamentally altered my perception of the Japanese economy. I had been bullish for a long time, not only because of the high growth rate it achieved in the post-war period, but also because Japan's leaders appeared to be able to adapt to difficult circumstances. When I saw that this was no longer the case, I lost confidence in policymakers' ability to tackle deflation, and I refrained from recommending investments in Japan throughout my tenure as Chief Investment Strategist at J.P. Morgan Private Bank.

Conclusions

Diagnosis of Problem
The key issue for investors was to decipher whether Japan's real estate and stock market surge in the second half of the 1980s was a bubble. While it is obvious in hindsight, most investors at the time concluded that the run-up in asset prices was justified by low interest rates and the seeming resilience of Japan's economy to a super-strong yen.

Policy Response
The bubble burst when the Bank of Japan tightened monetary policy in the early 1990s and kept interest rates high, well after the bubble burst. Policymakers failed to realize that deflation was becoming a threat until it was too late. Japan's problems were compounded when US officials pressed for a stronger yen, even though it contributed to deflation and did little to rectify the trade imbalance with the USA.

Market Response
Japan's stock market and real estate values both plummeted; yet, the yen continued to strengthen until the mid-1990s. Twenty years later, both markets are still well below the levels attained in the 1980s.

Portfolio Positioning
Following the bursting of Japan's bubble, I refrained from recommending Japan's stock market for the next two decades, because I lost confidence in the ability of policymakers to overcome deflation.

Notes

1. Ezra Vogel, *Japan as Number One*, originally published in 1979, now available through iUniverse.
2. See Christopher Wood, *The Bubble Economy: Japan's Extraordinary Speculative Boom of the '80s and the Dramatic Bust of the '90s*, Solstice Publishing, December 2005. The book contains a discussion of Japanese accounting and regulatory treatment that contributed to extensive problems in the financial sector.
3. Wood notes that Japanese banks borrowed extensively in the Eurodollar market, and that even though they were the largest banks in the world, they had to pay a premium that was called the "Japanese rate."
4. One factor that made real estate highly illiquid was that the Japanese government established high taxes on land to discourage speculation, with land held less than two years subject to a 150 % capital gains tax.
5. See Jesper Kohl, J.P. Morgan Securities Ltd., "Japan Without the 'Hidden' Safety Net," October 28, 1997.
6. Wood, *The Bubble Economy.*
7. Richard Koo, *The Holy Grail of Macroeconomics: Lessons from Japan's Great Recession*, John Wiley, revised edition, August 2009.
8. Benjamin Bernanke, Federal Reserve Board, "Deflation: Making Sure 'It' Doesn't Happen Here," November 21, 2002.
9. Salomon Brothers, International Bond Market Analysis, report dated June 15, 1988.

8

Asia's Real Estate Boom Triggers Global Contagion

Since the breakdown of Bretton Woods, the countries in Emerging Asia have been among the fastest growing in the world, which has been a topic of interest for international economists. Nonetheless, until the mid-1990s these economies were not a focal point of US international economic policy. This mainly reflected the small size of many countries in the region, as well as their ability to perform on their own during the less developed countries (LDCs) financial crisis of the 1980s.

Since then, several developments coalesced to bring Emerging Asia to the attention of US officials and the public at large. The most publicized was China's emergence as an economic superpower in the past decade (this is discussed in Chap. 11). However, the key development that required international policy coordination in the late 1990s was the Asian financial crisis. It surfaced when Thailand was forced to devalue the bhat in mid-1997, and currency pressures spread to other parts of Southeast Asia and later to North Asia and other parts of the world.

The Asian crisis is noteworthy because it marked the first time that financial contagion swept the globe—and there was controversy at the time about what caused it. Some officials in the region blamed international investors for precipitating the turmoil, and several prominent economists questioned whether developing countries should maintain open capital markets: Indeed, some argued that capital controls were necessary to prevent recurrences. For inves-

Portions of this chapter are based commentaries I wrote in April 1999 while I was Chief Investment Strategist at J.P. Morgan Private Bank, and in September 2005 while I was Chief Investment Officer at Fort Washington Investment Advisors.

tors, it posed the question of how a problem in a small country—Thailand—could spread from Southeast Asia, to North Asia and then to other parts of the world.

Apart from contagion, the Asian crisis is also significant for investors, because it marked a new type of crisis confronting emerging economies. Unlike "old-style" foreign exchange crises—in which deficit financing by governments and accommodative monetary policies were at the root of the problems—balance-sheet positions of property developers and financial institutions contributed to the severity of the Asian financial crisis. The International Monetary Fund (IMF) was criticized by some economists and Asian officials for exacerbating the situation by recommending policies that threatened the banking systems in several countries. At the same time, international investors faced the added challenge of having to assess how the financial systems would cope with higher interest rates.

In the aftermath, officials in the region concluded that the best defense against future crises was to run current account surpluses and accumulate foreign exchange reserves. There was also increased integration between Asian economies and the USA, in which the USA became a primary destination for Asian goods, while Asian central banks accumulated US debt at low interest rates. A key issue for policymakers and investors is whether this co-dependence is stable and durable. While critics believe the situation is fraught with risks and could unravel, I side with those who believe there are valid reasons for countries in the region to link their currencies to the US dollar.

The Allure of Emerging Asia

While there was considerable debate at the time about the causes of the Asian financial crisis, there was also general agreement that Asia's history of rapid economic growth, low inflation and sound economic policies made Emerging Asia an attractive investment haven:

- The five members of the Association of Southeast Asian Nations (ASEAN)—Indonesia, Malaysia, the Philippines, Singapore and Thailand—along with other Asian tigers such as Hong Kong, South Korea, Taiwan and China were considered the most dynamic economies in the world. They pursued export-led economic growth and maintained saving rates that were the highest in the world.
- They also had relatively low levels of external indebtedness and succeeded in overcoming external shocks in the 1970s and 1980s. During the debt

crisis of the 1980s, Indonesia and the Philippines were the only Pacific Rim countries to require IMF assistance, and both were considered success stories.

- The Asian countries were also perceived to be stable politically, although Thailand had frequent changes in leadership, and Indonesia faced uncertainty about the successor to President Suharto. The region also had a track record of currency stability. Until mid-1997, the only devaluation of any consequence in the previous ten years was a 20 % depreciation of the Philippines peso in 1990. Otherwise, annual currency fluctuations versus the dollar were fairly modest—typically 5 % or less.

Increased Reliance on Foreign Capital

Because of their high saving rates and reliance on export-led growth, Emerging Asia did not require significant external financing to sustain high economic growth in the 1980s and early 1990s. However, an investment boom in the property and real estate sectors of Southeast Asia left the region more dependent on foreign capital in the mid-1990s. The spending spree was particularly apparent in Thailand and Malaysia, where the rate of investment climbed above 40 % of gross domestic product (GDP) (see Table 8.1). South Korea also experienced an investment boom, as the Korean chaebols expanded their operations significantly.

The surge in investment resulted in a significant increase in the current account imbalances of four of the ASEAN members—Indonesia, Malaysia,

Table 8.1 Gross domestic fixed investment (% of GDP)

	1977–86	1987–96	1993–96
Emerging Asia	*25.4*	*29.3*	*31.5*
Excl. China	25.4	28.3	30.8
China	25.5[a]	30.5	33.2
Hong Kong	29.1	28.2	31.1
India	20.4	22.1	21.8
Indonesia	21.6	26.6	28.5
Malaysia	32.4	35.2	42.6
Philippines	23.1	21.1	23.2
Singapore	38.7	33.9	36.3
South Korea	27.6	35.1	37.2
Taiwan	21.9	22.3	23.9
Thailand	27.4	37.9	41.6

Source: J.P. Morgan
[a]1979–86

the Philippines and Thailand—and South Korea. In 1996, the combined current account deficit of this group reached $55 billion, or more than 5 % of their GDP. This represented a quadrupling of the combined deficit in four years, and it was accompanied by a steady increase in net private capital inflows.

The investment surge was financed primarily by commercial banks and finance companies in the region. These institutions funded themselves by taking on yen- or dollar-denominated loans from international banks, which were eager to expand exposure, especially when lending spreads surged during the Mexican peso crisis in 1994–95 (see Fig. 8.1). Net banking flows to the borrowers in Table 8.1 (excluding China and Hong Kong) surged from $33 billion in 1994 to $81 billion in 1996. Japanese multinationals, in particular, increasingly looked to Southeast Asia as an attractive place to establish operations, as Japan's economy failed to recover from the collapse of the 1980s bubble—and obtained ready financing from Japanese banks.

While the situation appeared to be stable, there were some signs of potential problems in the mid-1990s. The Asian equity markets underperformed other global markets after having doubled in 1993, and foreign purchases of equities were modest thereafter. By early 1997, international banks also turned cautious and limited new credit expansion to short-term loans when

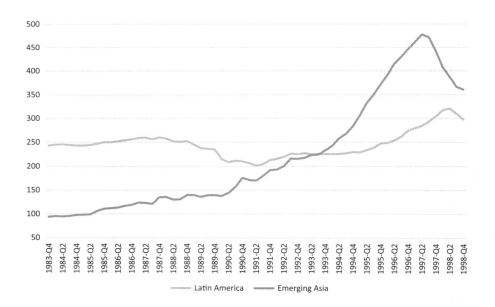

Fig. 8.1 Bank exposure by region ($ billion) (Source: BIS)

export growth slowed. As the property boom began to ebb, newspaper and magazine articles queried whether the Asian miracle was coming to an end, but it was difficult to tell whether the slowdown was cyclical or structural.

The Onset of the Crisis

The Southeast Asian crisis began with the devaluation on the Thai bhat on July 2, 1997. Thailand's financial markets initially rallied on the news, as investors believed the devaluation would improve the country's competitiveness and reduce its external deficit. However, the markets soon came under pressure, amid reports that Thailand's reserves were depleted and that Thai banks and finance companies faced increasing problem loans and rising debt serving costs.

It soon became clear that Thailand faced a dilemma: The country needed to maintain high interest rates to compensate investors for currency risks; at the same time, high interest rates threatened to undermine Thailand's weak financial system and create domestic debt problems. To break out of this trap, policymakers needed to take steps to improve investor confidence. However, the Thai government was too weak to act decisively, and the IMF stabilization package was inadequate. Furthermore, the USA was unwilling to come to Thailand's aid, as it did for Mexico in 1995. Lacking any reason to believe the situation would stabilize, investors began to pull funds out of Thailand.

By September, a similar chain of events was unfolding in the other ASEAN members with large external borrowings: One by one Malaysia, Indonesia and the Philippines were compelled to abandon their currency links to the dollar, and their financial markets suffered a similar fate as Thailand's, although the circumstances varied. Indonesia's problems were exacerbated by the rapid erosion of support for President Suharto and the poor design of the IMF stabilization program, which precipitated a banking panic. In Malaysia, investors lightened positions as the government blamed foreign speculators for the country's problems, rejected IMF assistance and eventually imposed capital controls. The cumulative impact of these developments was a shattering loss of investor confidence.

The Crisis Spreads

The fallout from these events on global financial markets was limited initially by Southeast Asia's small size, accounting for only 3–4 % of world GDP. Perceptions of the situation changed markedly in the fall of 1997, however, as the crisis spread to North Asia, engulfing financial markets in South Korea, Hong Kong, China, Taiwan and Japan. Developments in these economies proved harder to ignore, as they collectively represent about one-quarter of the world's output. Except for South Korea, the external conditions for North Asia were also vastly different from their ASEAN neighbors: Japan, Hong Kong, China and Taiwan were running a combined current account surplus of $130 billion in 1997; yet, their currencies and financial markets were under intense pressure (Table 8.2).

The currency pressures experienced by the North Asian countries partly reflected the loss of competitiveness versus Southeast Asia. Taiwan, for example, allowed its currency to depreciate, even though it was running a large current account surplus and had huge foreign exchange reserves. This development fueled speculation that the Hong Kong authorities would follow suit and abandon the fixed exchange rate to the dollar. As interest rates were bid up, property values in Hong Kong plummeted, and high-flying red-chip stocks began to crack.

More disturbing was the growing realization that Japan was headed for recession, which would exacerbate the deflationary forces spreading throughout Asia. As the largest economy in Asia, a Japanese upturn was critical to revive export growth throughout the region. Instead, Japan weakened in the first half of 1997, and it was just beginning to feel the fallout from the down-

Table 8.2 Financial indicators for Pacific Rim economies

	US$ fx rate (June 97=100)		Interest rates (% p.a.)		Stock prices (Dec 96=100)	
	Jun97	Jan98	Jun97	Jan98	Jun97	Jan98
North Asia						
China	100	100	10.1	8.6	109	71
Hong Kong	100	100	6.2	14.3	113	64
South Korea	100	55	11.5	23.0	115	77
Taiwan	100	82	11.5	7.7	130	112
ASEAN						
Indonesia	100	28	14.1	31.8	114	61
Malaysia	100	58	7.4	9.4	86	42
Philippines	100	63	10.8	20.1	82	54
Singapore	100	81	3.6	5.6	89	55
Thailand	100	47	20.0	26.0	64	44

Source: J.P. Morgan

turn in Southeast Asia in the second half. By year's end, it was evident that Asia was experiencing its worst crisis in the post-war era.

In 1998 the crisis spread beyond Asia, first to Latin America, where Argentina and Brazil faced currency pressures, and later to Russia, which was forced to devalue the ruble and, in August, to default on some government debt. By September, US financial markets felt the impact, when Long Term Capital Management, a prominent hedge fund, needed to be rescued. This development brought the Federal Reserve into play, as it lowered the federal funds rate by 25 basis points on three occasions. Markets shrugged off the first two moves, but the Fed was finally able to turn around market sentiment with its third rate cut. Thereafter, US and world financial markets sustained a strong rally that lasted into the early part of 2000.

The Role of International Capital Flows

Amid the turmoil triggered by a wave of currency depreciations, there was considerable controversy about the role international investors played, with the Prime Minister of Malaysia blaming them for what happened and then instituting capital controls for the country. Data compiled by Morgan's economists (see Table 8.3) indicate that the principal shift in capital flows for the eight countries in Emerging Asia was in international banking flows rather than securities transactions:

- Net bank loans swung from $81 billion in 1996 (3.2 % of GDP) to minus $84 billion in 1998.
- Net equity flows (stock transactions plus foreign direct investment) moderated from $65 billion in 1996 to $40 billion in 1998.
- Non-bank private creditors—a catch-all group that includes securities investors and finance companies—added slightly to exposure in this period,

Table 8.3 External financing: Emerging Asia (eight countries)

($ billions)	1994	1995	1996	1997	1998
Total equity, net	54	58	65	52	40
Total debt, net	51	88	111	56	−24
Public	17	9	4	29	28
Private	34	79	107	28	−52
Non-bank	1	14	26	25	32
Bank	33	65	81	3	−84
Medium and long term, net	35	43	63	95	29
Short term, net	16	45	48	−39	−53

Source: J.P. Morgan

as did official creditors (multilateral lending institutions, governments and export credit agencies).

These findings suggest there may have been little reason to impose controls on securities transactions: They were not a source of the build-up in external debt in the period leading up to the crisis, and Emerging Asian debt markets were relatively small and illiquid. Also, international purchases of Asian equities in the mid-1990s were modest, and any selling during the crisis period paled compared to the massive shift in banking flows. Indeed, most countries did not follow Malaysia's example of imposing capital controls, because they were perceived to be ineffective and also made it difficult to reattract foreign capital once conditions improved. To the extent that swings in international banking flows exacerbated the problems in the region, policymakers understandably looked for ways to dampen the volatility.

However, it is questionable whether this objective could be attained considering the recurring problems that developing countries encountered in the 1970s, 1980s and 1990s, despite numerous attempts by official and private institutions to formulate early warning systems. My experience is that these systems did not work, partly because critical information was missing or inaccurate, and the nature of the problem differed among countries and regions. Indeed, many of the external debt indicators that were relevant for Latin America did not signal problems for Emerging Asia, because Asia had relatively low external debt.

Rather, the problems in Asia were rooted in the property markets and domestic financial institutions, which fueled the asset bubble. In this context, some observers contend that recommendations by the IMF to stem currency attacks through tighter monetary policy were counter-productive, because higher interest rates exacerbated domestic debt problems and created massive problem loans (see Fig. 8.2). Also, because policymakers were unable to convince investors that they had an effective plan to rectify the situation, the currencies depreciated far more than was needed to maintain competitiveness and resulted in steadily widening interest rate differentials. This, in turn, created additional problems for banks and other institutions that borrowed in foreign currency.

Recovery from the Crisis

In the aftermath, the external balances of the Emerging Asian economies shifted into a sizeable surplus position. This occurred as investment rates among the ASEAN members, which had surged in the mid-1990s, fell back

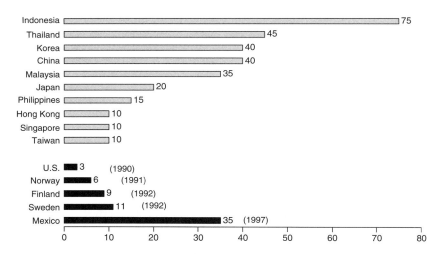

Fig. 8.2 Peak non-performing loans during banking crisis (% of total loans) (Source: Merrill Lynch/OECD)

to their previous rates, lessening import demand. At the same time, countries in the region gained a significant edge on their competition as their large currency depreciations boosted their exports and propelled economic growth in the region. The net result was the combined current account balance for Emerging Asia swung by $220 billion, from a $40 billion deficit in 1996 to a $180 billion surplus in 2004.

This shift accounted for 40 % of the increase in the US current account deficit over this period (Table 8.4). Including Japan, whose current account surplus has grown to more than $170 billion, there was a swing of $325 billion for the Asia-Pacific region.

At the same time, there was an even greater build-up in the foreign exchange reserves in the region. Including Japan, Asian central banks contributed more than $1.7 trillion—or 80 %—of the $2.2 trillion increase in global foreign exchange reserves from 1997 to 2004. Among the Emerging Asian countries, China accounted for the largest accumulation—an increase of more than $500 billion.

In a paper presented in 2005, Ben Bernanke, then a governor of the Federal Reserve, maintained that the ability of the USA to finance a record current account deficit (6 % of GDP in 2005) on favorable terms was a consequence of a "global saving glut."[1] He linked the build-up in official reserves by countries in the region to a desire to protect themselves from capital outflows. Because most Asian countries link their currencies, formally or informally, to the dollar, a majority of the build-up in their reserves represented purchases of US bonds.

Table 8.4 Global current account positions (in billions of dollars)

	1996	2004	Change
USA	−120	−666	−546
Euro area	78	53	−25
Japan	66	172	106
Developing:	−90	326	416
Latin America	−39	8	47
Middle East and Africa	1	74	116
Asia	−41	180	221
China	7	56	49

Source: "The Global Saving Glut and the US Current Account Deficit," remarks by Governor Ben S. Bernanke, April 14, 2005

Is the US–Asian Relationship Sustainable?

While the USA benefitted from the foreign central bank purchases of US debt, most economists at the time did not believe that the large payments imbalances could persist. First, no other industrial country had been able to sustain a current account deficit of 6 % of GDP, because it implies a debt build-up that is considerably faster than the growth of the economy. A second concern was that rapid accumulation of dollar reserves could lead to higher inflation in the Asia-Pacific region if central banks were unable to sterilize (or offset) the impact on domestic money supplies. Third, Asian central banks also were at risk of incurring huge foreign exchange losses if they allowed their currencies to appreciate against the dollar.

Proponents of the "Revised Bretton Woods II System" (BWII), however, contended that the Asian countries perceive benefits from linking their currencies to the dollar and, in effect, have resurrected a new fixed-exchange-rate system.[2] The crux of their argument was that the Emerging Asian economies formed a periphery in the international monetary system that was comparable to the role Europe and Japan played in the 1950s. The authors of the BWII view argued that this arrangement was stable and could be maintained.

Such optimism, however, was not shared by several prominent luminaries. Paul Volcker, Robert Rubin, George Soros and Warren Buffett, to name a few, contended the imbalances were unsustainable and fraught with risks.[3] In 2002, Warren Buffett began to short the US dollar for the first time. In 2005, Nouriel Roubini and Brad Setser warned that disputes over the imbalances could lead to a "hard landing" in 2005–06.[4] (Note: While some commentators later claimed they foresaw the 20008 crisis, their arguments were based on external payments imbalances being unsustainable rather than on problems with the safety and soundness of domestic financial systems.)

Thus far, at least, the dire outcome has not materialized, partly because there have been factors that mitigated the risk of a full-fledged dollar crisis. One factor is the ongoing desire of Asian central banks to tie their currencies to the US dollar. Some observers believe the principal motive for China and other Asian countries to maintain ties to the dollar is mercantilist—that is, a desire to promote exports by maintaining an undervalued currency. However, it is also important to remember that these countries tried to keep their pegs to the dollar in the second half of the 1990s, when the dollar was strong.

A second mitigating factor is the credibility the Federal Reserve has earned over the past two decades as an inflation fighter. The commitment of the Fed to keep US inflation low is critical to maintaining investor confidence in the dollar. In contrast, the breakdown of the Bretton Woods system in the early 1970s was preceded by rising US inflation and a massive build-up of dollar reserves by European central banks. The reserve build-up then ultimately contributed to higher inflation in Europe, and it created the perception in Europe that the USA was not a stable reserve center.

My own assessment is that because of the lack of a viable alternative to the dollar, it is natural for countries in Asia to continue to link their currencies to it. While this limits the ability of the respective countries to pursue monetary policies that are completely independent, they also derive considerable benefits from being linked to the US dollar, especially when their domestic financial systems are not well developed.

Ironically, one of the biggest challenges confronting investors today is the exact opposite of what policymakers worried about in the mid-2000s: Namely, the US dollar has strengthened considerably against most currencies as the Federal Reserve contemplates tightening monetary policy, which has caused the Chinese authorities to reassess exchange rate policy and allow the renminbi to soften against the dollar. Emerging markets have sold off, in turn, as investors are worried that China could be setting the stage for its currency to weaken further. (Note: This issue is discussed in more depth in Chap. 11.) This turnaround in fortunes vividly illustrates how circumstances can change completely from one decade to the next.

Perspective on the Asian Crisis

The Asian financial crisis merits important consideration by investors for several reasons. First, it illustrates how a seemingly small problem—a devaluation in Thailand—could spill over to neighboring economies in Southeast Asia, then spread to North Asia and Latin America, and eventually impact

US financial markets when Russia defaulted on its debt. No one at the time anticipated, or could have anticipated, such a chain of events. This same phenomenon, moreover, was also evident in the eurozone crisis that began in 2010 when problems in a small country—Greece—ultimately threatened the viability of the entire eurozone region.

Apart from financial contagion, the Asian crisis is also significant because it marked a new type of crisis confronting emerging economies. In a paper written in 2001, Rudiger Dornbusch distinguished "old-style or slow motion crises" that involved the financing of current account imbalances of financially repressed economies, and "new-style" balance sheet crises of financially open economies.[5] The main distinction is that the newer-style crises involve "doubt about the credit worthiness of the *balance sheet* of a significant part of the economy – private or public – and the exchange rate," and the capital account plays a key role in the run-up to the crisis and in its unfolding:

> The central part of the new-style crisis is the focus on balance sheets and capital flight. Balance sheet issues are, of course, fundamentally linked to mismatches; even if there were solvency there would be vulnerability related to liquidity problems. Exchange rate depreciation, in a mismatch situation, works in an unstable fashion to increase the prospect of insolvency and hence the urgency of capital flight.[6]

One implication is that "new-style" crises are more complex than "old-style" ones, which involve a cycle of overspending and real currency appreciations (due to high inflation and maintenance of fixed exchange rates). Thus, whereas the standard policy solution for the latter entails a combination of higher interest rates and currency depreciation to produce a reduction of real wages, such policies are likely to destabilize financial markets when capital markets are free and there is a mismatch between assets and liabilities of financial institutions. Dornbusch points out that trying to time "new-style crises" is inherently more difficult than ones where there is significant currency overvaluation and escalating current account deficits, because net capital inflows cover up the hole in bad balance sheets and transparency is absent. At the same time he points out that the proverbial straw can break the camel's back:

> A relatively minor event might upset a precarious refinancing scheme, or a suspicion raised in one part of the world might cause investors to kick the tire in another part of the world.[7]

Finally, Dornbusch identifies two key concerns in these circumstances. One is that the value at risk is extraordinarily large as a result of the interaction of mismatches in balance sheets. The other is that governments have a difficult time adhering to stabilization programs when a meltdown is under way. In this respect, the Asian crisis has aspects of both a currency crisis and an asset bubble.

Conclusions

Diagnosis of the Problem
The Asian crisis arose when countries in Southeast Asia borrowed extensively from abroad to finance a boom in commercial real estate. While it began with the devaluation of the Thai bhat, currency pressures spread quickly throughout the region and then to North Asia before reaching Latin America and Russia. This marked the first experience with global contagion since the developing country debt crisis in the early 1980s, and it caused policymakers to question how they should respond to highly volatile international capital.

Policy Response
Asian officials initially responded in traditional fashion to the attacks on their currencies by raising interest rates and borrowing from the IMF. This stance backfired, however, when banks in the region encountered funding problems, and tight credit and rising interest rates caused domestic assets to plummet in value. The predicament was compounded when their currencies depreciated by record amounts, which boosted the cost of their liabilities that were denominated in dollars or Japanese yen. Ultimately, Asian policymakers concluded that the best way to deal with this volatility was to reduce dependence on foreign capital and to build an arsenal of foreign exchange reserves.

Market Response
Investors responded to the crisis by selling Asian currencies indiscriminately, producing the worst financial crisis in the region in the post-war era. Banks, in turn, responded by reducing loan exposure to the region.

Portfolio Positioning
The Asian crisis occurred while I was the Chief Investment Strategist for J.P. Morgan Private Bank, when I made one of the worst calls of my career by recommending investors buy stocks in the ASEAN region. I misdiagnosed the

situation in Southeast Asia, mainly because I had been bullish on the region throughout my career and thought the poor showing of stocks in the region represented a buying opportunity. In particular, I did not realize the extent to which commercial real estate was being financed through international borrowing by banks in the region. Once I became aware of this, I was able to anticipate that the currency depreciations in Southeast Asia would put pressure on currencies in North Asia and other parts of the world.[8] From this perspective, it was a classic example of learning from your mistakes.

Notes

1. Remarks by Governor Ben S. Bernanke, "The Global Saving Glut and the US Current Account Deficit," April 14, 2005.
2. Michael P. Dooley, David Folkerts-Landau, Peter Garber, "An Essay on the Revised Bretton Woods System," NBER Working Paper 9971, September 2003.
3. Paul A. Volcker, "An Economy on Thin Ice," *Washington Post*, April 10, 2005.
4. Nouriel Roubini and Brad Setser, "Will the Bretton Woods 2 Regime Unravel Soon? The Risk of a Hard Landing in 2005–2006," First Draft, February 2005.
5. Rudiger Dornbusch, "A Primer on Emerging Market Crises," NBER Working Paper 8326, June 2001.
6. Ibid., p. 2.
7. Ibid., p. 6.
8. Note: I offered this assessment when I appeared on *Wall Street Week with Louis Rukeyser* in November 1997.

9

The Tech Bubble: Some Lessons for Rational Investors

The second half of the 1990s proved to be remarkable, following a lackluster start to the decade, for both the US economy and the stock market. The catalyst was a revival in productivity growth that accompanied advances in computer technology and more widespread application of the internet. Commentators in the media heralded it as the beginning of a new era in which the "old economy" founded on manufacturing would be displaced by a new tech-oriented economy. The US stock market initially surged on the back of strong corporate profits. However, by the end of the decade the market's advance far outpaced earnings growth, and valuations as measured by price to earnings multiples climbed to record levels for tech stocks.

Amid these developments, there was an ongoing debate between those who believed the stock market was priced efficiently and those who thought it was irrational. The Federal Reserve chairman Alan Greenspan initially sided with the skeptics. However, he subsequently modified his stance when he maintained the Fed's role was not to forecast bubbles, but to supply ample liquidity to financial markets after a bubble burst. The Fed did so when the economy weakened and the stock market plummeted by 50 % in the 2000–2002 period. While these actions helped to contain the fallout from the market's decline on the economy, critics of the Fed contended this policy response contributed to the ensuing bubble in US housing.

The popular impression is that investors collectively were caught up in "tech mania," which Professor Robert Shiller of Yale University in his book *Irrational Exuberance* (2000) attributed to human psychology and biased media coverage. My own take is that Shiller's explanation may be valid for retail investors who became enamored with the market's rise and for momen-

© The Editor(s) (if applicable) and The Author(s) 2016

121

N.P. Sargen, *Global Shocks*, DOI 10.1007/978-3-319-41105-7_9

tum investors who are trend followers. However, this does not tell the full story, as it ignores a significant group of investors who bucked the trend either by shorting tech stocks or by investing in value stocks that were out of favor. The problem they encountered was that the tech surge was too powerful and lasted too long for them to retain assets under management: The challenge these managers confronted was whether to stay true to their investment disciplines or to cave in and become closet indexers.

Backdrop for the "New Era" Mindset

Throughout the post-war era up to the mid-1990s, real economic growth in the USA averaged about 3.5 % per annum with two distinct periods. The first was the post-war recovery from 1948–73, in which real gross domestic product (GDP) growth averaged 4 % per annum. This was accompanied by labor productivity growth of nearly 3 % per annum. The second was the period following the first oil shock until the mid-1990s, when the pace of economic growth moderated to 3 %, as labor productivity growth fell by half to 1.5 %.

Just when it seemed the economy was on a steady-state trajectory, US economic growth suddenly accelerated to 4 % per annum in the second half of the 1990s, matching the pace achieved in the post-war recovery. This acceleration surprised most observers at the time, considering economic performance had been disappointing at the beginning of the 1990s. The fall of the Berlin Wall and the ensuing collapse of the Soviet Union had created optimism that a "peace dividend" associated with diminished need for defense spending would catapult the economy. However, when Iraq invaded Kuwait in summer 1990, oil prices spiked and the economy slipped into recession amid uncertainty about the outcome. While the recession was short-lived, the USA experienced a jobless recovery in 1991–92, and it was not until 1993 that it regained momentum. Even then, it was not clear what was to follow, as the Federal Reserve tightened monetary policy aggressively in order to contain inflation pressures, and long-term bond yields surged to 8 %. This caused the economy to falter at the beginning of 1995.

Behind the scenes, however, the groundwork was being laid for a revival of US productivity growth based on advances in computer technology that included development of smaller and faster micro-processors, sophisticated software and fiber optic networks. All of these, in turn, gave rise to widespread use of the internet. During the 1990s the growth rate of real investment in high-tech equipment and software accelerated, and it averaged nearly 24 % per annum in the second half of the decade (see Table 9.1),[1] and

Table 9.1 Changes in real investment and prices for IT (Average annual change %)

	1990–95	1995–2000	2000–03
Real investment			
IT	17.2	23.8	3.9
Software	12.6	19.1	1.8
Computers	33.2	35.6	18.3
Non-IT	4.8	4.4	−2.7
Price			
IT	−6.2	−7.8	−4.8
Software	−2.7	−0.5	−0.9
Computers	−14.8	−21.0	−14.3
Non-IT	1.9	0.4	1.3

Source: BEA, Federal Reserve Bank of San Francisco

by the end of the 1990s investment in information-processing equipment and software exceeded 3 % of GDP compared with 1 % at the beginning of the decade. At the same time, business equipment and software spending rose from 7 % of GDP at the beginning of the 1990s to 10 % at the end of the decade.[2]

According to a study by Mark Doms of the Federal Reserve Bank of San Francisco, much of the increase in IT investment in the late 1990s appears to be attributable to falling prices of IT goods, which made them more afford-able for end users.[3] However, Doms also finds that IT investment in 1999 and 2000 was much higher than his econometric model would predict. He concluded that another reason for the high growth rates in IT investment was that expectations were too high, especially in two sectors of the economy—telecommunications services and the dot-com sector.

The investment boom in this period is widely regarded as a key factor that boosted labor productivity growth to a 2.5 % annual rate in the second half of the 1990s. As the productive potential of the economy increased, it trans-lated not only to faster economic growth and lower unemployment, but lower inflation, as well: Over this period the economy posted real economic growth rates of 4–5 %; the unemployment rate fell from 6 % in 1994 to 4 % by the end of the decade; and the core rate of inflation fell from 3 % to 2 %. Headline inflation, as measured by the consumer price index, was even lower, as oil prices plummeted throughout the decade and fell to a low of $10 per barrel.

The absence of inflation pressures meant the Federal Reserve was not com-pelled to raise interest rates to slow the economy. In fact, it eased monetary policy on two occasions—during the Mexican peso crisis in the first half of 1995 and also during the turmoil surrounding the collapse of the hedge fund Long-Term Capital Management (LTCM) in September 1998. It was not until the following year that the Fed embarked on a program of policy tightening.

Stock Market Surge 1995–98

Against this backdrop, the stock market began what would be a five-year surge in the middle of 1995. Over the next three years, the S&P 500 composite and the NASDAQ composite both doubled in value. Two years later, by March 2000, the S&P 500 had risen by an additional 50 % and its level of 1500 was roughly three times higher than its value at the beginning of 1995. Meanwhile, the NASDAQ index had surged an additional two and a half times, and at its peak around 5000 was five times higher than its level at the beginning of 1995.

As the stock market advanced, there was an extensive debate between those who believed that valuations were too high and the market was mispriced, and those who maintained that the market's response was rational. A leading proponent of the former camp was Professor Robert Shiller, who maintained investors were caught up in a mania and market valuations were at extreme levels. His book *Irrational Exuberance* was a direct challenge to proponents of efficient markets, who maintained that valuations reflected the views of investors at the time who were incorporating all the available information. Shiller defined the term as follows:

> Irrational exuberance is the psychological basis of a speculative bubble. I define a speculative bubble as a situation in which news of price increases spurs investor enthusiasm, which spreads by psychological contagion from person to person, in the process amplifying stories that might justify the price increases.[4]

The debate centered on various measures of valuation that were used to ascertain whether the stock market was expensive, cheap or fairly valued. The metric that Shiller developed used the trend in cyclically adjusted price-earnings (CAPE) multiples over rolling ten-year periods. The logic was that this measure provided a basis for assessing normalized earnings over an economic cycle. It showed that the market value as of 1997 was a full standard deviation above the long-term average, and by March of 2000, it was several standard deviations higher. (Note: While Shiller's focus was the valuation of the broad market measured by the S&P 500 index, I later show that at the peak of the market, valuations for growth stocks were more than two times higher than for value stocks.)

The counter-argument was that Shiller's measure was based on backward earnings, and did not take account of the impact that technological change was having on boosting future earnings prospects. There was some credibility to this view in the 1995–97 time frame, when growth in corporate profits exceeded estimates of Wall Street analysts and strategists every year. From 1998 on, however, there was a noteworthy difference in the data on corporate profits reported by the national income accounts (which pointed to a slowdown) and those reported by companies to shareholders (which showed continued rapid growth in earnings).

Another argument that was advanced to justify an increase in valuations was that both inflation and interest rates had fallen to low levels, and that this development justified higher price–earnings (P/E) multiples. The model the Federal Reserve used to assess the stock market lent credibility to this argument, as it compared the earnings yield on the stock market (the inverse of the P/E multiple) to the yield on the ten-year treasury (see Fig. 9.1). Using this metric, the stock market did not appear to be significantly mispriced in the 1995–97 period: By 1997 the P/E multiple for the S&P 5000 composite

Fig. 9.1 The Fed model: S&P 500 earnings yield versus ten-year treasury yield (Source: Federal Reserve, Robert Shiller)

reached a level of about 16 times one year forward earnings, which was only marginally above the historic norm of 14–15 times earnings.

Amid this controversy, the major stock market indexes advanced fairly steadily, without a significant correction, until August–September 1998. US investors had previously shrugged off the Asian financial crisis on the grounds that the problem was far away and would not impact the US materially. However, perceptions changed when the crisis spread to Russia, which experienced sizeable capital outflows. The ruble plummeted as the country's holdings of foreign exchange reserves were depleted, and Russian government bonds sold off. When Russia defaulted on some of its debt, a flight to quality ensued in which risk assets were sold off worldwide while US treasuries and the dollar rallied.

As rumors circulated that LTCM, the prominent US hedge fund, was in trouble and on the brink of collapse, the S&P 500 index and the NASDAQ composite plummeted. This triggered worries among investors that the US economy was at risk if the sell-off continued and affected other financial institutions. Amid these developments, the Federal Reserve took steps to bolster investor confidence by lowering the federal funds rate. The first two cuts of 25 basis points each had little impact on stabilizing the financial markets. However, when the Fed lowered the funds rate a third time, investors greeted the move enthusiastically and shifted back into equities and other risk assets.

At the same time, the market response left many investors perplexed and confused: Why did the third rate-cut prove to be a charm, when the two previous ones failed to alter expectations? There was no clear answer to this question at the time. However, many investors concluded that this episode was another example of the so-called "Greenspan put," in which the Fed would ease policy whenever the stock market sold off significantly. Those who subscribed to this view added to their risk positions, taking comfort that the Fed would cover them if conditions worsened.

Market Frenzy: October 1998–March 2000

What ensued over the next 18 months made the market moves of the previous three years look tame by comparison: From October 1998 to the peak in March 2000, the S&P 500 index increased by about 50 % while the NASDAQ composite rose by more than 270 %, reaching a peak level of more than 5000.

During this period, investor optimism was fueled by developments in the technology sector that were linked to the turn of the millennium and commonly referred to as Y2K. The issue that investors latched on to was the need for businesses to replace software systems that might fail on January 1, 2000, because existing systems could not handle dates beginning with the year 2000. In anticipation of spending sizeable amounts of money to repair existing systems, many businesses moved forward capital spending plans to develop and purchase new, more sophisticated systems. Accelerated software investment plans spilled over to associated hardware spending, and they contributed to a surge in overall business investment. The mistake many investors made, however, was to project continued strong investment demand continuing into the next decade.

As the economy reaccelerated in 1999, economists and Wall Street analysts revised their projections for the economy and corporate profits steadily upward. Indeed, at the stock market's peak in March 2000, Wall Street analysts were projecting earnings growth for S&P 500 companies that would increase at a compound annual rate of 14 % per annum over the long term (See Fig. 9.2). This pace was nearly three times faster than the trend growth rate of the economy in nominal terms. The price earnings multiple for the S&P 500 index climbed to 24 times one-year forward earnings, a level that was nearly double the historic norm. (Note: For NASDAQ stocks, valuations reached levels that were substantially higher than for the S&P 500 index.) Once the bubble burst, analysts then revised their earnings projections steadily down-

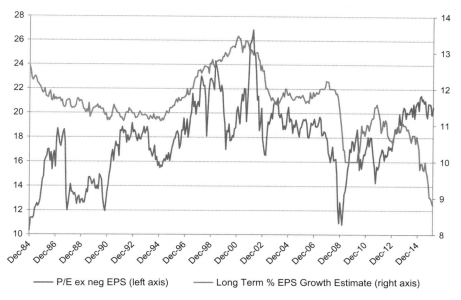

Fig. 9.2 US stock market valuation: a legacy of unrealistic earnings expectations (Source: Credit Suisse)

ward over time, and they are currently projecting long-term earnings growth in the high single digits.

Further justification for the stock market's relentless surge came from commentators who contended that the equity risk premium—or excess return for stocks over bonds—was too high. In a book entitled *Dow 36,000: The New Strategy for Profiting from the Coming Rise in the Stock Market*, two researchers at the American Enterprise Institute, James K. Glassman and Kevin Hassett, argued that the historic risk premium for stocks versus bonds of about 6 % was too high, considering that over sufficiently long time periods, returns for stocks were consistently higher than for bonds, and that the influence of market volatility diminished as the investment horizon is extended.[5] Their argument in a nutshell was that as long as investors had long-term investment horizons of 20 years or more, they could be reasonably confident that stocks would beat bonds handily. Therefore, as the equity risk premium diminished, Glassman and Hassett concluded the stock market was likely to continue rising in value. The projected level of 36,000 for the Dow assumed that the risk premium for equities was zero. (Note: The shortcoming in their argument is that investors may think they have a long-term orientation until the market sells off markedly, at which point they become short-term focused and run for the door.)

By mid-1999, the Federal Reserve took note of the economy's strength and began tightening monetary policy. Even as interest rates rose, however, investors were able to find reasons for purchasing stocks, especially those in the tech-telecom-media (TMT) space. One view that gained adherence was that the Fed's efforts to supply excess reserves to the banking system in the period leading up to the start of the millennium meant that this injection of liquidity had to find a home, and the most likely place would be in the stock market. The fallacy with this argument was that the reserves were simply held by the banks as a precaution against possible Y2K disruptions, rather than being used to back new loans. Nonetheless, many investors failed to grasp the distinction.

By late 1999, the market was experiencing an all-out buying frenzy. One illustration is that Merrill Lynch issued a research report on Qualcomm calling for it to triple in value over the next five years. The market's response was a doubling in the share price in the next three months! At the same time, Wall Street analysts were publishing reports recommending dot-com companies that had no meaningful earnings, and they developed new metrics for valuing companies based on the number of "hits" for their websites. The ability of individual investors to trade their own portfolios via the internet also gave rise to the phenomenon of "day traders," who managed their positions very actively.[6]

The Bust Sets In

The euphoric mood continued into the beginning of 2000, as Y2K proved to be a non-event. However, doubts about the stock market began to set in when the economy showed signs of moderating from its super-charged pace in the second half of 1999, and over the next three years the stock market posted its biggest losses at the time since the 1930s.

The sell-off occurred in three distinct phases. The first phase began in March 2000, when dot-com stocks began to plummet. For a while, investors shrugged this off as being inevitable considering how far prices had advanced. Later in the year, however, the network space began to weaken as well, when Cisco, which was the main supplier of routers to build out the internet, announced that revenue growth had slowed unexpectedly. This development caused investors to question whether the boom in business investment spending on technology was over. By year's end, the value of the NASDAQ composite had fallen by about 50 % while the S&P 500 index had declined by nearly 20 %.

The second phase of the sell-off occurred in 2001 amid signs that the US economy was faltering, as business capital spending turned negative. An added shock was the tragedy of September 11, which brought the USA to a standstill. Consumers pared back their spending amid the heightened uncertainty, and the economy slipped into a mild recession. By mid-September the NASDAQ had declined by nearly 70 % from its March 2000 peak, while the S&P 500 index was off by 32 %.

The third phase occurred in 2002, when yet another shock caused investors to lose confidence in the stock market. Among the key events were a series of accounting scandals that took down once prominent firms such as Enron and Arthur Anderson. These developments raised fundamental questions about the extent to which publicly traded companies were manipulating their earnings results to boost their share prices. Amid these revelations, the sell-off in the stock market broadened, and value-oriented companies that had previously withstood the sell-off witnessed declines in their share prices.

Further adding to investor doubts was the uncertainty about whether the USA would engage in conflict with Iraq over alleged weapons of mass destruction. It lasted until March 2003, when US forces invaded Iraq and overthrew Sadaam Hussein. Once the outcome was resolved and the uncertainty lifted, the stock market rallied from its lows amid signs that the US economy was rebounding and the Federal Reserve was maintaining record low interest rates.

Fed Policy Response

In the run-up to the stock market sell-off, the Federal Reserve tightened monetary policy by raising the federal funds rate from 4.75 % in mid-1999 to a peak rate of 6.5 % by mid-2000. Thereafter, the Fed responded in classic fashion to the ensuing economic slowdown by lowering the funds rate in regular increments. Following the September 11 shock it quickened the pace, and by 2002 it had lowered the funds rate to a then post-war low of 1 %. This was consistent with Chairman Greenspan's philosophy of providing ample liquidity to financial markets after an asset bubble burst, and the policy response helped contain the fallout, as no major financial institutions confronted insolvency.

The Federal Reserve, nonetheless, did not accomplish all of its objectives, as the economy failed to improve materially, and the jobless picture was troubling. At the same time, inflation had fallen below the Fed's 2 % target, and some observers began to express concerns that the USA could fall prey to deflation just as Japan did. These fears proved to be unfounded, however, as the economy recovered in 2003, and the decline in economic output during the recession was modest—less than 1 % of GDP. One of the principal reasons is that the financial system was not heavily exposed to a decline in tech stocks.

The Fed's actions at the time were widely viewed as being successful in terms of dampening the fallout after the tech bubble burst. However, William White, who was then chief economist for the Bank of International Settlements, contended that the monetary authorities needed to take account of the importance of financial stability in setting monetary policy. In an address before the Kansas City Federal Reserve Symposium in Jackson Hole in August 2003, White urged central banks to take into account the effects their low interest rate policies could have on fostering asset bubbles, and he concluded it was appropriate for central banks to lean against the wind when asset prices were rising rapidly.[7]

The Federal Reserve and other central banks ignored these warnings, however, and the US economy gained strength in 2004. By 2005, it was clear the economy had regained momentum, and asset prices had recovered most of the value lost during the 2000–02 time period. However, the seeds were being sown for a massive expansion of credit that fueled an unprecedented rise in housing prices.

Lessons for Investors

In many respects the technology bubble is a classic example of how asset bubbles are formed and the way they typically play out. The initial surge in stock prices was fundamentally based on much stronger-than-expected earnings. Prospects for the US economy had improved as a result of technological change in computer hardware and software that led to widespread application of the internet. This translated into increases in corporate profits that exceeded investor expectations, and which left valuations, while somewhat elevated, within a reasonable range. The stock market also experienced a significant pullback in the third quarter of 1998 in response to worries about financial contagion.

Thereafter, a buying frenzy set in when the Federal Reserve eased monetary policy on three occasions to stabilize the market, and when investors as a group lost sight of valuations. During this phase, momentum on investing reigned supreme, as price increases begot further increases. In these circumstances, it is common for retail investors to flock to funds that posted the best returns; Shiller's book on irrational exuberance highlighted the role that the media played in boosting investor expectations. As shown in Fig. 9.3, at the peak in early 2000 the P/E ratio for growth stocks in the S&P500 index reached 40 times earnings, or more than two times greater than that for value stocks in the index.

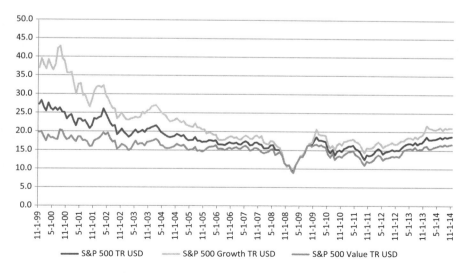

Fig. 9.3 P/E ratios for growth and value stocks in the S&P 500 index (Source: Morningstar)

During the sell-off phase, the pitfalls of momentum investing became apparent, as value-style investing came back into favor: From March 2000 to September 2001, value indexes were relatively flat while the NASDAQ index declined by 70 %. Thus, value stocks, which lagged growth stocks during the bull-run, outperformed significantly in the early 2000s.

This begs a fundamental question that is at the crux of the debate about market efficiency—namely, how did so many professional investors get caught up in the buying frenzy? Did they base their decisions on optimistic reports by Wall Street analysts when it was widely known they were incented to market offerings that were underwritten by their firms? Or were they merely caught up in competitive pressures, where they risked underperforming their peers if they abstained from buying hot stocks?

My own assessment is that the latter force was extremely powerful. First, it is important to recognize that some prominent value investors were not caught up in the mania, and chose to hold cheaper "old economy" names in their portfolios. Moreover, some hedge fund managers attempted to short some of the high-flying tech companies, but ultimately had to close their shorts when they lost money doing so.[8] Indeed, the power and duration of the tech rally caused several successful money managers, including Julian Robertson and Gary Brinson, to exit the business of managing other peoples' money. Another prominent firm, Grantham, Mayo, Van Otterloo & Co., stayed the course and was eventually vindicated for calling the market a bubble. In the meantime, however, the firm suffered $10 billion of net client withdrawals during 1997–2000.[9]

For those investors who believe markets are efficient and that index positions are appropriate, it should also be recognized that passive investing helped magnify the overshoot: Such funds automatically increase the weightings of stocks that appreciate the most. Jeremy Grantham noted this trend and lamented the following:

> The industry has reached a point where career risk and business risk dominate the investment process. You can no longer manage money with an eye towards absolute risk, the way you would for your parents. Concerned with the risk of underperforming their benchmark, managers are tailoring their portfolios to track their index, plus or minus, a few minor adjustments. As a consequence, the arbitrage mechanism across asset classes has weakened considerably and markets are becoming quite inefficient.[10]

This is reminiscent of John Maynard Keynes' well-known saying "Worldly wisdom teaches that it is better for reputation to fail conventionally than to succeed unconventionally."

Changing Perceptions of the Tech Bubble

As I reflect upon this experience, what stands out the most is how my perception of the situation shifted over time as developments unfolded. When I joined J.P. Morgan Private Bank at the beginning of 1995, I had expertise in bonds and currencies, but not in making calls on the stock market. Therefore, my inclination was to be cautious, and I began by advising clients to expect stock market returns close to the long-term average of 10 % per annum. When the market significantly outperformed over the next three years, I did not believe it was mispriced, because corporate profits far exceeded expectations, which I called "the profits revolution." This was a way of saying that US businesses had become very adept at generating sustained profitability.

However, my view of the market shifted in 1998, when corporate profits as reported by the national income accounts showed a decline. I regarded the US government's statistics as being more reliable than pro-forma estimates reported by companies, because they are based on income tax filings and companies would incur huge fines if they fudged the numbers. I also took into account the impact of the contagion that was spreading around the world and thought it could eventually spill over to the USA.

I made a call mid-year that the bull market was over, and for a while it looked prescient when the failure of LTCM caused the market to crater. However, when the market reversed course following the Fed policy easing in September, I opted not to stand in the way of a freight train and became "neutral" on the market. Note: This is what portfolio managers do to survive when they are not sure what is happening! My strategy was to lie low until the market had turned, at which time I made a call that tech stocks were excessively valued and there was better value in neglected sectors of the market. This turned out to be a good call, as value stocks far outperformed growth stocks over the next three years.

During 2002, the broad market capitulated as the accounting scandals associated with Enron, Arthur Anderson and other firms led to a complete loss of investor confidence in the markets. My view was that the sell-off was excessive and that a catalyst was needed to provide the spark. This occurred in early 2003 when the USA invaded Iraq and overthrew Sadaam Hussein, and the stock market rebounded once the cloud over Iraq was lifted.

In the end, what I learned from this experience is that it is hard to detect bubbles in advance, because they are formed when conditions are favorable and they can build over a long time period. Accordingly, it is risky for an investor to take on a market that has considerable momentum. In my view, it is better to limit the damage when this is happening and not make big bets, so you have the wherewithal to take advantage of an eventual turn in momentum. This requires investors to be patient when the market moves against them, which it is never easy to do.

Conclusions

Diagnosis of the Problem

During the second half of the 1990s investors had to decide whether a surge in the stock market led by tech stocks was reasonable based on prospects for the "new economy" or a bubble spawned by irrational exuberance. The initial run-up in the stock market from 1995 to 1997 was supported by better-than-expected corporate profits. However, profit growth slowed in 1998 and a true buying frenzy took hold after the Federal Reserve eased monetary policy three times in September 1998. Also, some investors mistook spending by businesses on technology related to Y2K to be indicative of long-term trends.

Policy Response

Fed Chairman Greenspan discussed whether the stock market was subject to irrational exuberance in late 1996. However, he subsequently backed away from making a call on the stock market; instead he claimed that monetary policy should be directed at alleviating problems once a bubble burst. This stance contributed to "moral hazard," as investors viewed the Fed as being willing to protect their positions when the market sold off significantly.

Market Response

The S&P 500 index generated annual returns of more than 20 % for five consecutive years, with only one noteworthy pullback during summer 1998. The bubble burst after the Fed tightened monetary policy and profit growth fell short of expectations, especially for tech companies. The events of September 11, 2001 caused the market to plummet further, and a series of accounting scandals led to a broad-based sell-off in 2002.

Portfolio Positioning

The main challenge that value investors faced during the bubble was how to survive it, as portfolio managers who resisted the rally in tech stocks underperformed their benchmarks, lost assets and in some instances exited the money management business. For many investors, this experience validated Keynes' observation that markets can stay irrational longer than you can stay solvent.

Notes

1. Mark Doms, "The Boom and Bust in Information Technology Investment," Federal Reserve Bank of San Francisco, 2003.
2. Alan Beckenstein, "The New Economy," Darden Business Publishing, October 7, 2009.
3. Doms, "The Boom and Bust in Information Technology Investment".
4. Robert Shiller, *Irrational Exuberance*, Princeton University Press, 2002, p. 2
5. James K. Glassman and Kevin A. Hassett, *Dow 36,000: The New Strategy for Profiting from the Coming Rise in the Stock Market*, Times Business, 1999.
6. William White, BIS, "Wither Monetary and Financial Stability? The Implications of Evolving Policy Regimes," presented at Jackson Hole, Wyoming, August 28–30, 2003.
7. An interpretation based on behavioral finance is there are "limits to arbitrage." See Miguel Herschberg's article in *Palermo Business Review*, No. 7, 2012.
8. Andre F. Perold and Joshua N. Musher, Harvard Business School, "Grantham, Mayo, Van Otterloo & Co., 2001," March 18, 2002.
9. Ibid.
10. Ibid, p. 13.

10

The Global Financial Crisis: No Place for Investors to Hide

The global financial crisis and Great Recession was a milestone event that ushered in the third phase in the evolution of the international financial system following the Great Inflation of the 1970s and early 1980s, and the Great Moderation that followed and lasted through 2007. While there were bouts of financial instability that required periodic interventions by Group of Seven (G-7) policymakers during the second phase, the general impression at the time was that the world's financial system was fundamentally sound.

This image was shattered by the events that unfolded during the 2008–09 global financial crisis, which triggered the worst recession in the post-war era and the collapse of several prominent financial institutions. Policymakers took unprecedented actions to stabilize the financial markets and spawn economic recovery, but global economic growth was at its weakest in post-war history. Moreover, the threat of deflation became a concern in Europe as well as Japan in the wake of the eurozone crisis. Some observers contend that the environment of low growth and minimal inflation is here to stay and have dubbed it "The New Normal."

This chapter investigates the forces that gave rise to this transformation, starting with the bubble in the US housing sector and the role played by abundant credit and securitization in spreading exposure to low-quality mortgages throughout the US economy and other parts of the world. We then consider the actions that are being undertaken to prevent a recurrence, and present reasons why increased regulation of financial institutions is unlikely to diminish the prospects for future asset bubbles and financial market turmoil.

The chapter also highlights some of the major challenges investors faced in navigating through the crisis, including lack of transparency about balance

© The Editor(s) (if applicable) and The Author(s) 2016
N.P. Sargen, *Global Shocks*, DOI 10.1007/978-3-319-41105-7_10

sheet positions of financial institutions, which made it difficult to discern the degree of leverage and inter-connectedness in the financial system. Once these problems became apparent, there was a virtual free-fall in asset values around the world, and portfolio diversification provided investors with little or no protection. The choice they faced was to hold on to positions in financial assets that were plummeting in value, or to sell them and add to cash positions, treasuries or gold. Amid all this, investors schooled in the tenets of modern portfolio theory and efficient markets had little to guide them.

Origins of the Financial Crisis: A Bubble in US Housing

The origins of the global financial crisis are well known by now.[1] They are generally traced to a bubble that formed in US housing from the mid-1990s to 2006, in which national home prices more than doubled in nominal terms and rose by more than 50 % when adjusted for consumer price inflation (CPI) less shelter (See Fig. 10.1). The rise in housing prices was not uniform. It was greatest in fast-growing areas in California, Nevada, Arizona, Florida and the East Coast, where demand growth outstripped supply, and was modest in the Midwest, where available land was plentiful.

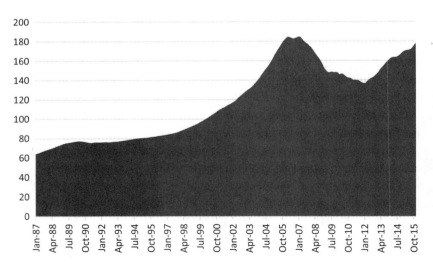

Fig. 10.1   US home prices (Source: National Association of Realtors)

One of the main factors contributing to the price surge was the widely held belief that homes were a safe investment that did not go down in value, and which offered the prospect of material appreciation. In a 2003 survey Carl Case and Robert Shiller reported that the vast majority of respondents agreed with the statement that real estate is the best long-term investment, and respondents expected future price increases of 6–15 % per annum, depending on the location.[2]

In addition, low interest rates and readily available mortgage financing made home purchases more affordable for borrowers. Prior to 2000, lending to subprime borrowers was virtually non-existent, but it took off exponentially thereafter, as lenders devised a host of products to make mortgages more affordable. They often solicited first-time homebuyers who did not put down any money on their home, and who were not even required to verify their income or assets (known as Alt-A and Alt-B mortgage-backed securities). Lenders were encouraged by the strong showing of subprime loans made during 2001–05, and the low interest rate environment contributed to the largest volume of home refinancing.

Accompanying these changes was the ongoing evolution of securitization, in which mortgages were pooled into packages and securities were then sold in various tranches to end buyers. Beginning in the 1970s the two main government-sponsored enterprises, Fannie Mae and Freddie Mac, developed this financing technique using "conforming" loans for prime borrowers while adding their guarantees to these mortgage-backed securities (MBSs). During the 1980s the private sector developed MBS backed by non-conforming loans, but the market stayed relatively small until the late 1990s, when commercial and investment banks developed new ways of securitizing lower-quality mortgages. This entailed the creation of collateralized debt obligations (CDOs), which included tranches of MBS and pooled them with other asset-backed securities (ABSs). Another development was the creation of credit default swaps, which allowed purchasers to buy protection against the risk of default by the seller. While CDS offers a form of insurance, there is no guarantee that in the case of default the seller will have adequate funds to make full payment, such that there is still counter-party risk.

These new financial instruments thrived in an environment of easy credit, poor regulatory oversight and generous ratings from the various credit-rating institutions. The alleged appeal of these securities was that they purportedly helped to diversify risks. In fact, they became vehicles for disseminating risks throughout the financial system. As the Brookings article by Baily et al. observes:

> What is especially shocking, though, is how institutions along each link of the securitization chain failed to perform adequate risk assessment on the mortgage related assets they held and traded. From the mortgage originator, to the loan servicer, to the mortgage-backed security issuer, to the CDO issuer, to the CDS protection seller, to the credit rating agencies, and to the holders of all those securities, at no point did any institution stop the party or question the little-understood computer risk models, or the blatantly unsustainable deterioration of the loan terms of the underlying mortgages.[3]

In short, in addition to a bubble in housing the origins of the financial crisis can be traced to flaws in the way in which mortgages were originated, packaged and distributed to end purchasers of MBS, and which contaminated the entire financial system.

Problems in Housing Spread

Accompanying the surge in home prices was an ample supply of credit that made borrowing costs inexpensive. This was apparent in the bond market, where credit spreads versus treasuries fell steadily from 2003 and approached record lows in 2006. By early 2007, there were growing signs that home price appreciation was slowing, and news stories about problems with subprime mortgages proliferated. Credit markets, nonetheless, remained calm through the spring and early summer, despite reports about increased delinquencies in the subprime space. By June, both Moody's and S&P began to downgrade certain tranches, and Bear Sterns announced trouble at two of its hedge funds that invested in MBS.

Amid these developments the Federal Reserve sought to reassure the populace that the problems with subprime mortgages were very manageable. In testimony to Congress in July, Fed Chairman Bernanke estimated that losses associated with subprime credit problems could be in the range of $50–$100 billion. While problems in the housing sector posed a risk to the economy, the Fed did not foresee a recession; in fact, Fed forecasts called for the economy to reaccelerate in 2008.

Perceptions among investors shifted materially in early August in the wake of several developments, including bankruptcy filings by the two troubled Bear Stearns hedge funds and problems with French insurer AXA's money-management business and with German bank IKB Deutsche, which had exposure to US subprime loans. On August 9, investors were shocked to learn that the European Central Bank and Federal Reserve had increased liquidity to banks in response to a seizing up of credit markets that triggered a liquidity crisis. It occurred as institutional investors and firms refused to renew sale and repurchase agreements (repo) with their financial counter-parties.

Many investors learned for the first time that commercial banks had set up off-balance sheet entities called "special investment vehicles" (SIVs) that invested in asset-backed securities and which funded themselves by borrowing in the commercial paper market. These entities effectively allowed commercial banks to leverage their balance sheets while the entities issued short-term debt to fund purchases of illiquid instruments.

Credit spreads widened significantly for the first time since 2002 (Fig. 10.2), and they continued to rise through to the end of the year, as did the LIBOR–OIS (London Interbank offered rate–overnight index swap) spread, which is a measure of interbank counter-party risk (Fig. 10.3). The Federal Reserve responded by cutting the discount rate by 50 basis points to 5.75 % in mid-August and one month later lowered the funds rate by the same amount to 4.75 %. Thereafter, the Fed lowered the funds rate after each Federal Open Market Committee (FOMC) meeting, through to the end of the year.

These actions helped calm markets in early 2008, but there were increasing signs that the economy had weakened at the end of 2007, and econo-

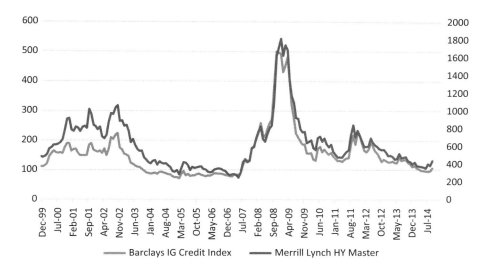

Fig. 10.2 Credit spreads versus treasuries (in percentage points) (Source: Barclays, Merrill Lynch)

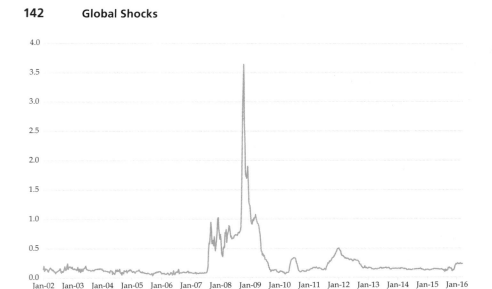

Fig. 10.3 LIBOR-OIS spread (in percentage points) (Source: Federal Reserve)

mists began to forecast a mild recession for 2008. Meanwhile, estimates of the potential losses associated with subprime mortgages, including Alt-A and Alt-B MBSs, rose to about $400 billion.

Amid these developments, markets were jolted further in mid-March by the announcement that Bear Stearns was being sold to J.P. Morgan Chase for $2 a share under an arrangement brokered by the Federal Reserve and the US Treasury. This transaction was enhanced by a $30 billion loan guarantee from the Fed, which marked the first time it provided support to an investment bank. The de facto bankruptcy, in turn, fueled rumors that Lehman Brothers and Merrill Lynch were also vulnerable. To reassure the markets, the Federal Reserve lowered the federal funds rate by a full percentage point in March–April to 2 %, but the issue that many investors pondered was whether this would be enough to stabilize the situation.

Panic Sets In

By late summer, it was increasingly apparent that actions by policymakers were not having the intended effect, as problems surfaced with both Fannie Mae and Freddie Mac related to their holdings of lower-quality MBSs. In early September, Treasury Secretary Paulson announced that both institutions would be placed in conservatorship, which would enable them to fulfill their financial obligations. This action was deemed critical to assure foreign entities that held their obligations, because they assumed they carried the full faith and credit of the US government.

These efforts proved to be too little, too late, however, when policymakers allowed Lehman Brothers to fail. In its wake several money markets "broke the buck" on their net asset values, as there was a run on mutual funds that held Lehman commercial paper, and credit markets seized up, as worries spread about other investment banks—including Merrill Lynch, Morgan Stanley and Goldman Sachs—that could be next. The concerns about counter-party risk are particularly evident in the spike in the LIBOR-OIS spread shown in Fig. 10.3. When credit markets seized up, many institutions responded by deleveraging their portfolios, and by necessity they often were compelled to sell higher-rated instruments where there was market liquidity.

The US Treasury and Federal Reserve attempted to contain the fallout as the Fed pumped liquidity into the financial system while the Treasury developed the Troubled Asset Relief Program (TARP) to purchase illiquid assets held by financial institutions. Goldman Sachs and Morgan Stanley, in an attempt to stabilize their liquidity, changed their charters to become commercial banks.

One of the purposes of TARP was to increase the liquidity of the secondary mortgage markets via government purchases of illiquid residential mortgage-backed securities (RMBSs). The program, however, failed to mollify the markets when it became apparent that the global economy was falling into severe recession, and investors shunned risk assets in favor of holding cash, gold and treasuries. By mid-March 2009, world equity markets had lost nearly 50 % of their value while high-yield bonds sold off by more than 25 %.

To stabilize the financial markets US policymakers undertook decisive actions that included large-scale purchases of financial assets as the federal funds rate approached the zero boundary, while the US Treasury converted the TARP program into one where the proceeds were used to recapitalize financial institutions. The latter action helped to alleviate worries that major financial institutions were technically insolvent, and in April investors drew comfort that stress tests of the leading financial institutions showed a smaller capital shortfall than had been anticipated. Financial markets rallied on this news, and by midyear there was growing evidence that the US economy was emerging from a severe recession.

What Made the Crisis So Severe?

The short answer is that the financial system was far more complex and inter-connected (domestically and globally) than most observers realized. Over the past three decades, commercial banks had shifted capital investments away from portfolio lending models toward originate-to-sell models based on securitization. Accompanying this transformation was the evolution of a parallel banking system—so called shadow banks—consisting of entities such as hedge funds, SIVs, special purpose entities (SPEs), money market funds, repo-markets and other non-bank financial institutions.[4]

Because so-called "shadow banks" do not take deposits they are subject to less regulation than traditional banks; yet they are inter-related with traditional banks via credit intermediation and securitization. Many observers, including New York Federal Reserve President Geithner, attributed the freezing of credit markets in summer 2008 to a run on entities in the shadow banking system by their counter-parties. These linkages within the US financial system, more-over, extended to financial institutions abroad, especially to European institutions that acquired significant holdings of US mortgage-backed securities.

While the 2008–09 global financial crisis is widely regarded as the worst crisis since the Great Depression, Professor Gary Gorton of Yale University observed that it was not like previous panics in US history "in that it was not a mass run on banks by individual depositors, but instead was a run by firms and institutional investors on financial firms."[5] During the 1930s, for example, the failures of a large number of small and mid-sized banks collectively caused the money supply to contract by 30 %. By comparison, the problems in 2008 arose from the failure, or near failure, of many of the largest invest-ment banks and commercial banks. Today, these institutions are classified as "systemically important financial institutions," or SIFIs, and are commonly regarded as "too big to fail."

The institutions that became troubled had three common attributes. First, virtually all of them had a high percentage of "toxic assets" on their books. In an environment of low interest rates and narrow margins, these institutions were eager to provide securitized mortgages and other structured products that boosted fee incomes. While they off-loaded most of what they structured, they held on to some senior tranches, believing they were secure.

Second, at the same time, these firms sought to boost overall profitabil-ity via excessive financial leverage. Investment banks increased debt levels to 30–40 times equity capital with the tacit blessing of the US Securities and Exchange Commission (SEC), and commercial banks created off-balance sheet entities to increase leverage, with the Federal Reserve permitting them to do so. Other institutions that were part of the "shadow banking system" were also exposed to the housing sector but did not have access to central bank liquidity or Federal Deposit Insurance Corporation (FDIC) guarantees.

Third, the troubled institutions financed long-term holdings with very short-term borrowings. The trigger for disaster was that the value of their assets plummeted when the housing bubble burst, and the impact was magnified by the need to de-lever their balance sheets quickly at fire-sale prices. When Lehman Brothers failed, investors began liquidating money market funds and banks no longer accepted counter-party risks, causing credit markets to come to a standstill. Households and corporations, in turn, were forced to reduce their indebtedness, which sent the global economy into a severe downturn.

In the ensuing period, there was an extensive debate about how long it would take for economies to recover. Initially, some forecasters maintained that the US economy would mirror the "V-shaped" rebounds that were common in the post-war era. However, research by Carmen Reinhart and Vincent Reinhart found that retrenchments following a severe financial crisis often take a decade, and the economic growth rate is a full percentage point below the long-term trend rate.[6] Today, it is clear that these warnings were very pertinent. Since recovery began in mid-2009, the US economy has grown at just over a 2 % annualized rate, well below the average for previous recoveries and the long-term trend rate of more than 3 %.

What Can Be Done to Prevent a Recurrence?[7]

This is the most contentious issue today, as there is considerable disagreement about the roles that various agents—financial institutions, regulatory and supervisory bodies, the rating agencies and policymakers—played. In the wake of all that transpired, government officials sought to reassure the public that they would take steps to insure that the problem will not be repeated.

Toward this goal the Financial Crisis Inquiry Commission (FCIC) was formed to investigate the causes of the crisis and to make recommendations to enhance the safety and soundness of the financial system. In its report published in February 2011 the majority view was that the crisis was a culmination of a bubble in housing and a breakdown in the process of securitizing mortgages. As the report states, "it was the collapse of the housing bubble – fueled by low interest rates, easy and available credit, scant regulation, and toxic mortgages – that was the spark."[8] The majority view believed the crisis could have been averted if the USA had adopted more restrictive regulations in conjunction with more aggressive regulation and supervision.

The FCIC also issued a dissenting view that interpreted the crisis very differently.[9] The minority view observes that the USA was not the only country to experience a credit bubble, as many European countries were afflicted as well. It criticizes the majority opinion for "focusing too narrowly on US regulatory policy and supervision, ignoring international parallels, emphasizing only arguments for greater regulation, failing to prioritize the causes, and failing to distinguish sufficiently between causes and effects."[10] According to the dissenting view, "global capital flows and risk re-pricing caused the credit bubble, and we consider them essential to explaining the crisis. US monetary policy may have been an amplifying factor, but it did not by itself cause the credit bubble, nor was it essential to causing the crisis."[11]

Well before the FCIC's report was released, however, Congress passed the Dodd-Frank Act in mid-2010, the most comprehensive legislation of the financial system since the Glass-Stegall Act in the 1930s. Many of the goals seem laudatory: providing better consumer protection from abusive financial practices, ending "too big to fail" bailouts, creating an early warning system, and improving transparency and accounting for exotic instruments. The main problem with Dodd- Frank, however, is its complexity—849 pages of legislation and several thousand pages in subsequent rule-making documentation.

Although the primary objective of Dodd-Frank is to make another financial crisis less likely to occur, many question whether it will succeed. The banking industry, for example, has become even more concentrated, with the top five US banks today accounting for nearly half of all deposits, as compared with 30 % ten years ago. At the same time, Dodd-Frank imposes significant new restrictions on the activities of many banks, insurance companies and other financial institutions that had little to do with the crisis. Consequently, some fear it could result in regulatory overload.

The alternative is a more targeted approach, such as the Basel III proposal to increase minimum requirements for bank capital and liquidity. This approach seeks to eliminate excess leverage in the financial system, which was a key factor contributing to the crisis and its severity. For example, Kim Schoenholtz notes that even if all of the nearly $2 trillion in outstanding subprime debt in 2007 had become worthless, the loss of wealth would have been equivalent to a stock market decline of less than 8 %: "The reason that subprime debt mattered so greatly is that *the losses sat on the balance sheets of leveraged intermediaries.*"[12] Addressing this issue, therefore, is central to restoring the safety and soundness of the financial system.

Turning to monetary policy, it is difficult to identify policy changes that are directed at financial stability. Prior to the 2008 financial crisis, the prevailing view in the economics profession was that asset bubbles were difficult, if not impossible, to predict, and advocates of efficient markets challenged the very concept of an asset bubble. Fed Chairman Alan Greenspan maintained that policymakers should not attempt to burst an asset bubble, but should be prepared to mop them up by providing ample liquidity to the financial system. This approach became known as "The Greenspan put."

In the wake of the fallout from the financial crisis, Federal Reserve and Treasury officials now pay greater attention to regulatory oversight of individual institutions and to macro-prudential issues that affect the stability of the financial system as a whole. These efforts are certainly welcome and are long past due. However, it is difficult to identify any changes in the conduct of monetary policies that are directed at financial stability. Indeed, the Federal Reserve and other central banks have pursued unorthodox monetary policies to keep interest rates near zero. While the Fed's strategy is designed to foster greater risk taking to bolster the economic expansion, it also has distorted prices in capital markets and could have the consequence of creating yet another market bubble.

At the end of the day, one has to decide whether it is appropriate to view the 2008–09 financial crisis in isolation, which is the approach used to justify Dodd-Frank, or to view it in a broader context, as yet another example of the growing number of crises that have impacted the global economy in the past 30 years. What is interesting about these experiences is that they occurred during a period of economic strength and low inflation. As William White, former economic advisor at the Bank for International Settlements (BIS), has argued, central banks viewed their overriding mission as restoring the low inflation environment that prevailed during the Bretton Woods era. But the context for setting monetary policies changed radically beginning in the second half of the 1970s, as financial deregulation and liberalization coincided with increasing capital market integration around the world. The end result was that US and European financial systems became highly leveraged and interconnected. Viewed from this perspective, monetary policies need to take greater account of the process of credit creation and the transmission of international capital flows via financial markets in order to lessen the risk of future bubbles.

Lessons for Investors

Finally, consider some of the key challenges that investors confronted leading up to and following the global financial crisis.

What made it so difficult for investors to anticipate the crisis? The prevailing view is that because a major financial crisis had not occurred since the 1930s, and policymakers were believed to be better equipped, market participants became overly complacent and believed large financial institutions were "too big to fail." While there is certainly validity to this argument, I contend that investors had to make three assessments to anticipate the crisis. First, they had to foresee the bubble in US housing prices. Second, they had to believe that credit was unusually cheap. Third, they had to anticipate the vulnerabilities in the financial system at home and abroad.

In my own case, I was correct about the first two assessments, as I believed US home prices were overvalued by 15–20% (rather than by 30 %+), and I thought credit spreads were too narrow. Yet, I did not foresee the vulnerability of the financial system. The reason: It appeared to be a "black box" and I trusted the regulatory bodies that had access on the exposures of individual institutions to detect any problems, but this trust was misplaced.

Fortunately, the US Treasury and Federal Reserve, along with international organizations such as the BIS and the International Monetary Fund (IMF), are now working diligently to improve the transparency of the financial system. This includes work to expand the scope and quality of data to analyze financial stability and to improve the analytical toolkit that risk managers use.[13] Nonetheless, while these initiatives should help to detect potential trouble areas in advance, I believe it is inherently difficult to time financial crises with any degree of precision.

A second challenge that the financial crisis highlighted is the difficulty of assessing the policy responses. When the subprime problem surfaced in the first half of 2007, the Federal Reserve continually reassured the public that the problems were small in the aggregate and were unlikely to spill over to the economy as a whole. Even as leading financial institutions began to fail, beginning with the collapse of Bear Stearns in early 2008, Fed and Treasury officials responded in piecemeal fashion. It was not until Lehman Brothers failed and other institutions needed to be rescued that policymakers understood the gravity of the situation and began to deal with the systemic risks.

Nonetheless, while officials were slow to grasp what was happening prior to Lehman, Fed Chairman Bernanke deserves credit for saving the financial system when it was on the brink of collapse, by supplying ample liquidity to

Table 10.1 Investment returns for various asset classes (in %)

	Panic (9/1/08–3/9/09)	Recovery (12/31/08–12/31/14)
Equities		
S&P500	−46.4	162.2
EAFE ($)	−49.4	81.4
EM($)	−48.7	110.1
Bonds		
Treasuries	6.4	20.8
Corporates (IG)	−5.5	67.0
High Yield	−26.0	157.2
EMBI ($)	−14.2	82.0
Commodities		
Oil (WTI)	−59.2	19.4
Gold	10.9	44.8

Source: S&P, MSCI, J.P. Morgan, IMF
Note: The March 9 date is when the low for the U.S. stock was reached. The recovery period is dated from the beginning of 2009, as bonds rallied before the stock market.

the financial system and being willing to pursue unorthodox monetary policies. Similarly, the stress tests of the US financial system conducted under the auspices of the US Treasury were vital to restore investor confidence in the financial system. Based on these policy responses, our firm was sufficiently reassured that we began adding to positions in investment-grade corporate bonds in December 2008 and then expanded our purchases into high-yield bonds and US equities in the first part of 2009.

A third challenge was the incredibly difficult environment for equity investors. Although the US stock market had risen to an all-time high by 2014, the path was a roller-coaster ride: After falling by 45 % in the six months through March 2009, the market rebounded by 75 % over the next 12 months, then gyrated in "risk on/risk off" mode for two years, before surging again for the next two years (see Table 10.1).[14] Virtually no one could have anticipated these twists and turns, and the majority of fund managers trailed their benchmarks. With the markets largely being driven by macro forces, conditions have been especially trying for portfolio managers who consider themselves to be bottom-up stock pickers. They have learned that they must pay attention to global macro developments or risk prolonged underperformance.

The fourth challenge was how to position portfolios during the panic phase when there was no benefit to being diversified. Investors faced the choice of clinging to corporate stocks and bonds that were plummeting in value or liquidating positions and holding cash, treasuries or gold. There was little to guide them in this period, and by the time markets had stabilized, in spring 2009, many were too shell-shocked to reinvest, even though many financial assets had become unduly cheap.

Conclusions

Diagnosis of the Problem
There is an ongoing debate today about the causes of the financial crisis. While it began in a small part of the economy—subprime debt for homeowners—the problem spread and infiltrated the US and global financial system. The severity of the crisis reflected the vulnerability of leading financial institutions to a decline in home prices owing to large holdings of "toxic" assets, a significant mismatch between the duration of their assets and liabilities that left them illiquid, and excessive leverage that rendered them insolvent.

Policy Response
As the crisis unfolded policymakers responded in ad hoc fashion to surprise developments and did not recognize the systemic nature of the problems. US monetary policy contributed to the crisis by making credit readily available on easy terms. Once the crisis became full-fledged after the failure of Lehman Brothers, the Federal Reserve under Chairman Bernanke pursued unorthodox policies that succeeded in stabilizing the financial system. In addition, the US government modified the TARP program such that it could be used to recapitalize the major financial institutions.

Market Response
US credit markets were the first to respond to the worsening of the subprime problem, which spilled over to money markets and European financial institutions by August 2007. While US and global equity markets advanced until October of that year, they plummeted in 2008 and early 2009, falling by about 50 %. The ensuing stock market rally began in March 2009, when investors became more confident that the financial system would survive, although bonds had begun to rally near the beginning of the year.

Portfolio Positioning
During the sell-off phase, there was no place for investors to hide other than holding cash, US treasuries or gold. During the rebound phase, by comparison, risk assets far outperformed safe assets, as US corporate profits recovered and the Federal Reserve kept interest rates near zero. The main lesson for me was the importance of staying flexible as the crisis unfolded and perceptions of it changed. The decision by our firm to redeploy capital, in turn, hinged on our assessment that valuations were at extreme low levels, and our confi-

dence that policymakers knew what to do to stabilize the financial system. Our firm's response to the crisis is spelled out in greater detail in Chap. 12.

Notes

1. For an excellent synopsis, see Martin Neil Bailey, Robert E. Litan and Matthew S. Johnson, "The Origins of the Financial Crisis," Business and Public Policy at Brookings, November 2008.
2. See Karl E. Case and Robert J. Shiller, "Is There A Bubble in the US Housing Market?" *Brookings Papers on Economic Activity*, 2003 No. 2.
3. Bailey et al., op cit. Note: more recently, there have also been a growing number of lawsuits against firms that underwrote mortgage-backed securities that misrepresented the collateral backing them.
4. See Gary Gorton and Andrew Metrick, "Regulating the Shadow Banking System," *Brookings Papers on Economic Activity*, fall 2010.
5. See Gary Gorton, "Questions and Answers about the Financial Crisis," prepared for the US Financial Crisis Inquiry Commission," February 20, 2010.
6. Carmen Reinhart and Vincent Reinhart, "After the Fall," NBER Working Paper no. 16334, September 2010.
7. I first discussed this issue in an article "Facing the Reality of Bubble Risk" in the *CFA Institute Magazine*, July/August 2014.
8. *The Financial Crisis Inquiry Report*, submitted by The Financial Crisis Inquiry Commission, January 2011, Official Government Edition.
9. See the Dissenting Statement of commissioners Keith Hennesy, Douglas Holtz-Eakin and Bill Thomas.
10. Ibid., p. 416.
11. Ibid., p. 421.
12. See Kim Schoenholtz's blog, *Money, Banking and Financial Markets*, "It's the leverage, stupid!" November 17, 2014.
13. See, for example, remarks by Richard Berner, Director, Office of Financial Research, US Treasury at the 14th Annual Risk Management Convention, March 12, 2013.
14. For further discussion see Nicholas Sargen, "Aftershocks," *CFA Institute Magazine* commentary, August 2013.

11

China's Economic Miracle: Will It Become the Next Bubble?

Not all shocks are bad. One of the most significant developments since the 1980s has been the emergence of China as an economic power. Following Mao Tse Teng's death, China embarked on a program of economic reforms in the late 1970s under the leadership of Deng Xiaoping that transformed it from a backward country into the world's second-largest economy today. Over that period, China grew at a compound rate of 9.5 % annually, and it has amassed record external surpluses in the past decade that turned it into the world's largest capital exporter. As such, China's economy now has considerable influence not only on other Pacific Rim economies but those in other parts of the world as well.

China's influence on the global economy and financial markets first became apparent in the decade beginning in 2000, when it propelled a boom in commodity prices that contributed to a resurgence in growth throughout Asia and other emerging economies. Subsequently, during the global financial crisis, China embarked on a huge stimulus package that lifted the Asian region out of a slump. More recently, however, China's economy has slowed below 7 %, and actions by policymakers to bolster the stock market backfired, causing global investors to be wary of its future.

Recognizing what has transpired and is at stake going forward, one of the most important decisions confronting investors is to make the correct call on the future of China. The challenge that investors face is sorting through varied opinions by China experts, which are often conflicting: They run the gambit from optimists who believe China will eventually overtake the USA as the

© The Editor(s) (if applicable) and The Author(s) 2016
N.P. Sargen, *Global Shocks*, DOI 10.1007/978-3-319-41105-7_11

world's most important economy, to pessimists who believe an asset bubble will spawn a financial crisis. Over the past decade I have devoted considerable time to assess which view is the most likely.

My starting point is to understand the development strategy that shaped the Chinese "miracle," and then to assess the key challenges that confront China's leaders in sustaining it. The most important are for the economy to evolve away from Japanese-style export-led growth to domestic-demand-led growth, and for the financial system to shift from one that is tightly controlled to one that is market-oriented. While both transitions are necessary, the risks that they could go awry have increased considerably, as is apparent from the recent growth scare. And while there is less risk of a run on the banks that are state controlled, an infusion of government funds would signal the extent to which resources have been poorly allocated, which in turn would heighten the risk of a growth recession.

Another issue that investors need to consider is how to play China. Previously, investment professionals favored a strategy of investing in emerging economies that supplied resources to China over a strategy of investing directly in Chinese equities, due to restrictions on foreign purchases as well as the influence the Chinese government exerts on state-owned enterprises and privately owned companies. While this "indirect" strategy worked very well in the past decade when commodity prices surged, emerging markets are now under assault as commodity prices have plunged in the wake of fears about China's growth.

Origins of the Chinese Miracle

The origins of China's economic miracle are rooted in a series of reforms that were implemented by Deng Xiaoping beginning in the late 1970s.[1] Deng's vision was to transform China's centrally planned economy into one that was more market-oriented, but which retained a prominent role for the central government in overseeing the evolution. The approach was to proceed by implementing a series of experiments with various sectors and studying the outcomes, rather than embarking on "shock therapy" as some Eastern bloc countries did after the collapse of the Berlin Wall. Collectively the impact of these reforms was to improve the overall efficiency of China's economy considerably.

Agricultural Reforms

Deng's starting point was the agriculture sector, which had been neglected by the Communist Party, and which had been a major disappointment for the Soviet Union as it attempted to modernize its economy. By the late 1970s, China was experiencing major shortages of food supplies and output, and some observers at the time warned that famines could kill millions of people. Deng responded by dismantling collective farms and by implementing the "household responsibility system," which divided the communal land into private plots, where farmers were allowed to keep their surplus harvest after paying state taxes.

These reforms were greeted enthusiastically by farmers, and agricultural output surged by more than 10 % per annum in the first half of the 1980s. Food price inflation plummeted, in turn, as output and productivity surged.

Industrial Reforms

Soon after the agricultural reforms bore fruit, Deng began to implement reforms designed to modernize China's industrial sector. They included liberalizing rigid price controls on industrial output, and allowing prices to be determined by market forces. At the same time, the authorities allowed worker's compensation to be tied more directly to their performance via a "piece work" scheme in an attempt to boost labor productivity. An effort was also made to decentralize the economy by allocating a larger portion of the central government's revenues to local authorities, which created incentives for them to develop local economies. A dual price system was established, where state-owned industries were allowed to sell production above plan quotas, and output was sold both at plan and market prices.

China was also opened to foreign investment for the first time under communist rule. A series of special economic zones were established for foreign investment that were relatively free of bureaucratic control, and in which the output could be exported. The province of Guangdong in southeast China was the first to be designated as a Special Economic Zone (SEZ). Based on its success other provinces along China's coast were granted similar status.

These efforts to modernize Chinese industry had mixed results initially. The main positive was that they succeeded in boosting industrial output and productivity. However, many of the state enterprises incurred losses, which acted as a drain on government finances. As the central government's budget deficit expanded, they became a source of inflationary pressures in the second half of the 1980s and early 1990s.

Increased Privatization

In the 1990s a new generation of leaders emerged, headed by Jiang Zemin as party leader and Zhu Ronji as premier, who was responsible for overseeing the economy. They observed that workers and managers were using state-owned assets to maximize their personal wealth rather than boost profits, and they concluded that a new set of reforms was needed in which increased privatization of former state-owned enterprises was pivotal. These reforms allowed for greater labor mobility, private ownership of housing, elimination of dual foreign exchange rate systems and encouragement of private sector investment in areas that were formerly controlled by the state.

As a result of these reforms, privatizations of state-owned enterprises accelerated throughout the 1990s and, by the mid-1990s, the private sector surpassed the state sector in terms of share of gross domestic product (GDP). This trend continued into the following decade and, by the mid-2000s, the Chinese economy was transformed into one where the private sector played an increasingly important role.

Internationalization

The crowning achievement at the beginning of the new millennium was China's admission to the World Trade Organization (WTO).[2] To become eligible, China had to embark on a program to reduce tariffs and other trade barriers. Throughout the reform period in the 1980s and 1990s the overall tariff rate fell from about 55 % to 15 %. Upon entry to the WTO, less than 40 % of imports were subject to tariffs and less than 10 % were subject to licensing and quotas.

The decade of the 2000s marked a turning point in which China's influence on the Asia-Pacific region and other parts of the world became highly visible. During the decade it contributed 20–30 % of global GDP growth, and its massive stimulus package during the 2008–09 financial crisis helped support recovery throughout the Asia-Pacific region.

Accompanying this was unprecedented growth in China's exports, which rose from about 3 % of world exports at the beginning of the decade to nearly 10 % at the end. There was also a major shift in the composition of exports, with those to emerging economies rising steadily and approaching half of China's export total, while the share to the Group of Seven (G-7) countries declined steadily, as China encountered growing trade frictions with the USA and Europe.

At the same time, China's import demand surged, especially for natural resources that were needed to power industrial development. China became a net oil importer in the mid-1990s and 15 years later it imported nearly half of its total oil consumption. Meanwhile, demand soared for raw materials such as iron ore, copper and coal, as well as that for other commodities. In the process China became a key driver of the so-called "super cycle" in global commodity markets: It currently consumes about 30 % of the world's commodities.

Prior to the 2008 financial crisis, China's current account surplus soared to a record 10 % of GDP, and its growing bilateral imbalance with the USA created trade frictions similar to those between the US and Japan in the 1980s (see Fig. 11.1) In the process, China supplanted Japan as the world's largest capital exporter, and its holding of foreign exchange reserves reached a peak of $4 trillion.

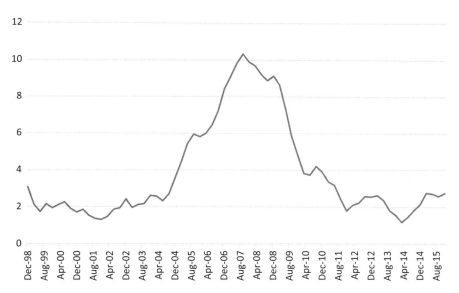

Fig. 11.1 China's current account surplus (% of GDP) (Source: IMF)

Stalled Reforms

While the success of China's transformation over the past 35 years is beyond dispute, policymakers also have encountered numerous challenges along the way, and there has been an extensive debate among China followers about how long the miracle can be sustained. One of the primary concerns that has been voiced is that China's export-led development strategy was modeled after Japan's, and it could suffer a similar fate if China does not achieve more balanced growth.[3]

For their part, China's former leaders, President Hu Jintao and Premier Wen Jiabao, were well aware of the potential consequences of weaker growth in the industrial countries. In 2008 Premier Wen discussed—in a speech that has been called the "Four Uns"—the rebalancing imperative that China faced. Wen observed that China's economy was strong on the surface but beneath the surface it was increasingly "unstable, unbalanced, uncoordinated, and ultimately unsustainable."

Subsequently, China's 12th Five-Year Plan that was formulated to cover 2011–15 called for transitioning the Chinese economy from export- and investment-led growth to greater reliance on domestic consumption. This occurred in a context in which personal consumption had fallen to a record low of about 35 % of GDP. The plan emphasized three ways to foster consumption-led growth, including boosting employment, raising wages and encouraging households to save less. The latter was to be achieved by strengthening China's modest retirement system, in which the lifetime benefits for the average Chinese worker averaged only $470.

Some prominent China watchers, however, were critical of the strategy under the Hu/Wen leadership. BCA Research, for example, argued that China's leaders had moved away from policies that emphasized economic efficiency, entrepreneurship, privatization and decentralization in favor of more populist policies:

> All of these issues represent serious challenges to China's economic health. But they are also symptoms of a much deeper problem: stalled economic reforms and waning momentum of broader restructuring efforts… The Chinese government must identify the root causes of these problems and confront the wide range of difficult economic and social issues that are inextricably linked to its growth. Otherwise, China's long-run growth could be in jeopardy.[4]

Current Reform Plans: A Delicate Balance

In the meantime, President Xi Jingping and Premier Li Keqiang became China's new leaders in late 2012, and they have confronted a host of issues. One of the biggest challenges is to embark on structural reforms that will improve the country's long-term prospects, while sustaining a growth trajectory of 6–7 % in the interim. The dilemma that China's leaders face is that many structural problems have worsened since the global financial crisis. The investment share of GDP, for example, has increased as a result of the fiscal and monetary expansion implemented to support economic growth (Fig. 11.2). According to research by Morningstar, China's investment boom is unmatched by any country on record:

> By any measure of fixed–asset intensity – growth rates, share of cumulative GDP growth, or share of GDP, China has far surpassed the precedents set by Japan, Korea and Taiwan. We estimate that, relative to the starting size of the economy, cumulative additions to Chinese capital stock in its boom decade have been 43 % greater than Japan's, 33 % greater than Korea's, and 49 % greater than Taiwan's.[5]

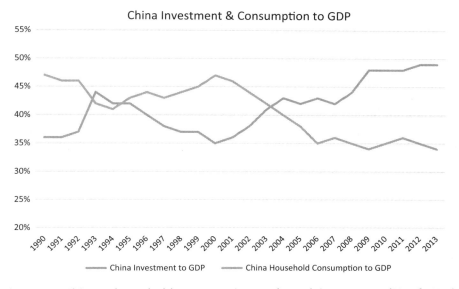

Fig. 11.2 Chinese household consumption and total investment (% of GDP) (Source: National Bureau of Statistics of China, IMF)

In this regard, the challenge that China's leaders confront in transitioning away from investment-led growth to consumption-led growth is even more daunting than other "miracle economies" faced.

Against this backdrop, the Chinese government announced a reform blueprint in November 2013 that would guide the country's development in the coming decade. Regarding economic reforms, the main breakthrough claimed by the Chinese leadership is that market forces would be granted the "determining" role in shaping the economy, while the government will recede to a supportive position. One of the unique features that contributed to China's extraordinary success was its "asymmetric market liberalization approach" during the reform period, in which there was nearly full liberalization of product markets while factor markets were heavily distorted.[6] Henceforth, the government claimed it would allow market forces to become the primary determinant of factor prices, as well. The three key areas affected include (1) pricing for financial markets, including interest rates and the value of the renminbi (RMB); (2) pricing resources such as water energy, transport and telecom; and (3) pricing of land, particularly in rural areas.

Of these, underpricing of capital is widely considered to be the most important form of distortion in China today. China has a comprehensive financial industry including various types of banks, securities firms, insurance companies and an array of money and financial markets. Interest rates were strictly controlled by the state during the early years of economic reform, and were set at low levels to subsidize investments. While interest rates were liberalized in the 1990s, financial markets remained underdeveloped, and deposit and lending rates of commercial banks remain low and are negative after adjusting for inflation.

One consequence is that large state-owned enterprises or foreign-owned private enterprises receive most of the bank loans, while small and medium-sized businesses often obtain funding from unregulated or "shadow" institutions. Interest rates in the curb market typically are well above those charged by commercial banks, and there has been rapid growth in this segment in recent years.

The controlled nature of domestic interest rates and the attempt by the authorities to set the exchange rate implies that financial markets often operate in disequilibrium. In the process, the authorities rely on capital controls and intervention to regulate the foreign exchange market and domestic credit allocation.

2015 Growth Scare

As of 2016, during this past year the tensions that China's leaders are encountering in finding the right balance became readily apparent, when the government actively encouraged domestic residents to buy shares of state-owned entities, when the economy was not performing to plan. However, this stance backfired when the stock market plummeted after it had risen by as much as 150 % in the year to mid-June. Officials responded by requiring state-controlled institutions to purchase stocks while at the same time suspending trading in more than half of publicly traded companies. This action, in turn, left market participants wondering if the government understood the consequences of its actions.

Subsequently, the Bank of China surprised market participants by announcing that market forces would be allowed to play a bigger role in determining the value of the yuan. When the yuan depreciated by 2 % on August 11, 2015, news reports declared it was the largest devaluation in more than two decades and that it threatened to set off a "currency war" if the yuan continued to slide. Thereafter, many emerging market currencies sold off significantly as the price for oil and other commodities sank, based on fears that China's economy was weakening more than the official statistics indicated. These developments, in turn, contributed to a worldwide sell-off in equities and other risk assets.

In light of these developments, some observers are questioning whether China's growth model is nearing an end. George Magnus, an associate at Oxford University's China Centre, concludes an article on that topic with the following observation:

> China's economic transition was always going to be difficult, but developments this year suggests that things are not going according to plan. The centralization of power is proving to be a double-edged sword for reform, the anti-corruption campaign is choking off initiative and growth and the economy cannot be kept on an unrealistic expansionary path by unending stimulus. The time for accepting permanently lower growth is drawing closer. It will test the legitimacy and reform appetite of China's leaders in ways that will determine the country's prospects for years to come.[7]

That said, the challenge for investors is to decipher whether China's economy is on a gradual slide path to achieve 5–6 % growth, or whether it could experience a growth recession in which the pace of economic activity plummets to 3 % or lower. In this regard, I view the recent scare as a "preview of coming attractions" for the following reasons: First, China's economy is a "black box" for most investors. While few believe the official statistics that show the economy grew at nearly a 7 % rate in 2015, it is hard to gauge what the true rate is, although some estimate it is closer to 4 % or 5 % based on hard data such as industrial production, electrical usage and exports.[8]

Second, the linkages between China's stock market and the domestic economy are limited. Since the stock market was created 25 years ago, for example, share prices have lost half of their value on three occasions; yet the economy was not severely impacted. One reason is that equities are not widely held by the public; consequently, the associated wealth effect is believed to be small to moderate.

Third, one of the main factors that unsettled markets was the announced change in China's exchange rate policy, which market participants viewed as an attempt to devalue the RMB. However, I believe China's leaders have no intent of starting a "currency war" and thus far the depreciation of the yuan has been inconsequential, amounting to less than 4 % (see note on currency wars at the end of this chapter). That said, further depreciation of the RMB is likely as the economy slows and monetary policy is eased further.

Finally, it should also be noted that, prior to recent developments, the primary concern that investors had about China was whether the country was at risk from a bubble in property prices. Researchers at the Bank for International Settlements (BIS) have identified this sector to have a potentially greater impact on economies than equity markets, mainly because real estate is typically purchased with leverage and financial institutions have significantly larger exposures to this sector than to equities. Currently, China and several other prominent emerging economies are atop the BIS watch list for asset bubbles, mainly because of the rapid expansion in credit that occurred in the wake of the 2008 global financial crisis. Recognizing this, there would be greater reason for concern if problems in the stock market spilled over to the property sector.

How Would a Chinese Bubble Unfold?

In the event that a bubble were to burst in China's property sector, investors need to consider how it might play out. One of the themes of this book is that it will primarily depend on the nature of the policy response and whether officials are able to restore investor confidence.

In this regard, my take is that a bubble in China would play out differently from the way Japan's bubble burst or how the Asian financial crisis unfolded.

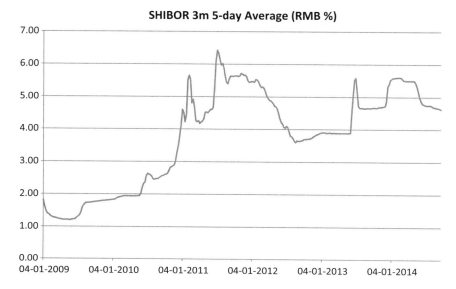

Fig. 11.3   Tight monetary conditions are being relaxed (Source: PBOC)

In both of those instances, policymakers responded by tightening monetary policies: In the case of Japan the central bank was worried about inflation when the real threat was deflation, and in the case of emerging Asia, policymakers were compelled to do so to stabilize their currencies. (Note: this is also true for several emerging economies today.)

By comparison, China's policymakers have already begun to ease monetary policy, and they are likely to continue to do so (see Fig. 11.3). This change is equivalent to a shift from the northeast zone to the southwest zone in the quadrant diagram, as monetary policy easing would likely be associated with a softening of the Chinese currency. Should interest rates fall to the zero boundary at some point, policymakers could consider quantitative easing. In this respect, the policy response would be similar to that of the USA in the aftermath of the bubbles in technology and housing. China has the freedom to do this because it has massive foreign exchange reserves and capital controls that allow it to follow an independent monetary policy.

Some observers also contend that if monetary policy stimulus fails to jumpstart the economy, China could embark on a new round of fiscal stimulus.[9] However, I am skeptical of this outcome, considering that the earlier programs increased financial leverage in China significantly: The ratio of domestic bank credit to GDP rose from 121 % in 2008 to 155 % in 2012.[10] This increase exceeds the 24 percentage point rise from 1994 to 1998, in which the ratio of non-performing loans in the banking sector subsequently surged to 30 %. The situation then required the Chinese government to inject public funds to restructure the major banks, including removing bad loans to asset management companies.

If anything, the situation today is more complex, because the fastest growth of credit has been outside traditional banking channels. This is apparent from examining the "total social financing" (TSF) statistics. They show that the share of bank loans has fallen from 95 % in 2002 to less than 60 % in 2012, while the share extended by trust loans, entrusted loans (entailing lending from one company to another through the banking system) and corporate bonds have increased significantly.[11]

The bottom line is whether it is reasonable to expect that banking sector asset quality will deteriorate significantly, owing to a combination of rapid growth in credit, high property values and weaker economic growth: The ratio of non-performing loans is little over 1 %. However, Professor Robert Z. Aliber, a renowned expert on asset bubbles, estimates the overhang of unoccupied apartment units is equivalent to 5–10 % of the urban housing stock, which could result in price declines of as much as 75–80 %.[12] In that event, he estimates the imbedded loan losses of the financial system could reach 20–30 % of bank assets.

A key difference from developed economies is that the Chinese government can make direct capital infusions into state-controlled entities, which effectively buys time for them to adjust. This does not mean that China would escape unscathed, however, as a bubble in the real estate sector and stock market is indicative of a misallocation of resources. According to Aliber, this could result in little or no economic growth during the workout phase.

How to Play China

Finally, whichever view one holds on China, investors need to determine the best way to express their view. The equity market is the typical channel that investors use to capitalize on an expanding economy. However, Chinese restrictions on capital flows and foreign ownership complicated the process and resulted in an array of markets, including the following ones:

- A-shares consisting of mainland–registered companies listed in Shanghai and Shenzhen that are denominated in RMB. This is the largest market, but foreigners are largely restricted from owning them.

- B-shares are denominated in US dollars and Hong Kong dollars and were created to attract foreign investors.
- H-shares are mainland-registered companies listed in Hong Kong and denominated in Hong Kong dollars. The main attraction of shares listed outside the mainland is adherence to more stringent regulatory requirements and accounting regulations.

Because of these complications, the most common way that foreign investors played China in the 1990s and the past decade was to do so indirectly—i.e., by seeking companies that provided resources, raw materials and services to fuel China's expansion. They included investments in major exporters of natural resources and commodities to China such as Australia, New Zealand, Argentina, Brazil and Chile. Other indirect plays were Japanese companies that shipped industrial machines for use in Chinese factories and financial service companies operating out of Hong Kong. This situation, in turn, gave rise to the acronym BRICs that was coined by Goldman Sachs to describe the growing importance of Brazil, Russia, India and China.

For the most part, this approach worked very well, as China's booming economy contributed to a secular boom in prices of natural resources and commodities. However, when China's economy slowed in the 2011–15 period, commodity process weakened substantially and there was accompanying slowdown in the growth of many emerging economies. In this context, the performance of the BRICs and other emerging equity markets trailed that of the developed markets considerably, after having outperformed materially in the prior decade (Table 11.1). Indeed, the 2015 growth scare highlighted the tremendous impact that a slowdown in China would have on primary producers and on countries for which China is a major export destination.

While there is no clear consensus about the prospects for emerging market equities today, the relevance of the BRIC concept for investors is increasingly being called into question by investment strategists. My own assessment is that it is a marketing concept rather than a legitimate investment theme,

Table 11.1 Annualized returns for BRICs versus S&P 500 index (in US dollars)

Market	2000–10 (%)	2011–15 (%)
China	9.2	0.9
India	14.7	−2.4
Brazil	18.8	−19.5
Russia	15.9	−11.9
BRIC Composite	13.8	−6.2
US (S&P)	0.4	12.6

Source: MSCI

considering the four economies are more heterogeneous than they are homogeneous. Indeed, China's emergence as a global superpower is by far the most important story, as its economy is greater than Brazil, Russia and India combined: Over the past decade its share of the world economy nearly doubled to 14 %, while the three other economies' shares have held steady at about 3 % each.

Should China embark on the reforms now being contemplated, in which there is freer flow of capital into and out of the country and domestic financial markets are liberalized, foreign investors would have more opportunity to play China directly. Otherwise, they are likely to refrain from investing in China on grounds that the cards are stacked against them. In the end, there are no shortcuts for investors in emerging markets other than to do extensive research on the risks, as well as the rewards, that each of them entails.

Conclusions

China's emergence as an economic power has been one of the most important developments impacting the global economy over the past 35 years. What happened to take the country from a backward economy to one of the most dynamic is truly remarkable, and China's transformation offers a counterpoint to the way that most developed economies have evolved. Notwithstanding this, however, there is a wide divergence in views about the country's future, ranging from those who are unbridled optimists to those who believe China is the next bubble that is about to burst.

Diagnosis of Problem
The debate about China's future illustrates some of the inherent difficulties detecting asset bubbles and trying to time them, as there have been dire warnings about the economy for the past two decades. While they proved to be false alarms, there are valid reasons to be concerned about potential financial turbulence resulting from excessive investment, high property valuations and rapid credit expansion. Indeed, the early warning system developed by the BIS suggests the situation warrants careful monitoring. However, even if a financial problem ensues, my assessment is it likely will play out differently than in Japan, Southeast Asia or the USA, because China's financial system is more directly controlled by the government.

Policy Response
China's policy response has been mixed. On the positive side, the government took steps to lessen the risk of a property bubble by limiting the number of

residences that a single owner can buy in major cities, and levying a new tax on real estate. However, the Chinese government has encountered challenges in fostering more balanced economic growth and in reforming the financial system. Whereas the reforms that were undertaken in the 1980s through to the early part of the 2000s improved allocative efficiency, the reform process has stalled since the mid-2000s and growth in productivity has dampened considerably. Also, the government's recent attempts to intervene directly in the stock market and to alter its exchange rate policy have resulted in a loss of investor confidence about its commitment to market-oriented reforms.

Market Response

Market participants are expecting the Chinese economy to slow gradually from the current pace of 7 %. However, substantially weaker growth of 3–4 % or less, which would constitute a growth recession, is not priced into markets. In this regard, the 2015 growth scare is a preview of how markets would react to a full-fledged weakening of China's economy.

Portfolio Positioning

The main challenge investors faced during China's boom was the primitive state of the financial system and the predominance of state-owned enterprises that made it difficult to invest directly in the country. Therefore, the strategy that most global investors deployed was to invest in "indirect plays" such as emerging economies that were suppliers to China. This strategy, however, has not worked as well in recent years, as China's slowdown and a weak global economy have lessened demand for commodities and raw materials. Going forward, therefore, investors will have to be more selective in determining the best opportunities.

A Note on Currency Wars

Since mid-2014, when investors began to anticipate eventual Fed tightening, the US dollar has surged against most currencies. For a while, China was one of the few holdouts that kept its currency tied to a strong dollar. However, the Chinese authorities wavered in August 2015, when they widened the band for the renminbi and allowed it to depreciate by 2 % against the dollar. Reports in the media heralded it as the biggest devaluation of China's currency in two decades, and pundits claimed that it threatened to lead to an escalation of "currency wars." Since then these fears have increased further as the Chinese authorities announced in December that they would henceforth peg the RMB to a basket of currencies, and the RMB subsequently weakened against the dollar.

My contention, however, is that such views not only distort what is happening, but they could exacerbate the situation if the strong dollar were to become a political issue in the USA. First of all, the recent wave of currency depreciations is not a result of countries deliberately weakening their currencies to gain a competitive advantage, such as occurred in the 1930s when "beggar my neighbor" policies were pursued. On the contrary, most countries have abstained from intervening in foreign exchange markets, and they have allowed market forces to determine the value of their currencies.

China is an outlier in this regard, as it has intervened heavily in foreign exchange markets to limit fluctuations of the RMB. In this case, however, China's central bank has been *selling* foreign exchange reserves, with its holdings of foreign exchange having fallen by more than $660 billion in the past year. This action has kept the RMB from falling as much against the dollar as market forces would have allowed. The reason: China's government is trying to counter capital flight from the country, which is estimated to have been in the vicinity of $1 trillion in 2015.

The Chinese authorities now find themselves in a quandary. The economy has slowed steadily for the past five years, which would normally have been accompanied by monetary policy easing. However, if they were to ease monetary policy now, they run the risk of being accused of trying to manipulate the country's exchange rate. (Note: US policymakers would like to see China stimulate its economy even if it means a weaker currency.) Meanwhile, Chinese officials reportedly are considering implementing capital controls to stem capital flight, which would allow them more flexibility to ease monetary policy.

While China has been the focal point about alleged "currency wars," one should not lose sight of how broadly based the dollar's appreciation has been since mid-2014, with the dollar's trade-weighted index having risen by about 25 %. Since then, the euro has fallen by about 20 % against the dollar, while the values of several prominent emerging market currencies have fallen substantially further. Depreciations for the Russian ruble, Brazilian real, Argentine peso and South African rand, for example, fall within a range from a high of more than 50 % for the ruble to 30 % for the rand.

Many commodity-exporting countries, instead of trying to defend their currencies against plummeting commodity prices, as they did in the past, have allowed market forces to determine the appropriate values for their currencies. The advantage of doing so is that it allows the exchange rate to cushion some of the decline in commodity prices that their exporters face, as each unit of dollar exports receipts translates into more local currency revenues. At the same time, the main risk is that large-scale currency depreciations have exacerbated inflation pressures in some countries—notably Russia and Brazil—such that their central banks have had to boost interest rates even as their economies have fallen into severe recessions.

In the end one may ask what all of this implies for the US economy as we enter the election period. My answer is that what is happening in markets today is very complex, and terms such as "currency wars" are misleading. In the aftermath of the global financial crisis, the US dollar was considerably undervalued in the period when the Federal Reserve lowered interest rates near zero and implemented several rounds of quantitative easing (QE). However, when the Fed signaled to the markets in mid-2014 that it was about to wind down QE and eventually tighten monetary policy, commodity prices plummeted and the dollar began to appreciate steadily. As of 2016, by comparison, the dollar appears to be somewhat expensive, as indicated by the softness in US manufacturing and the challenges that shale oil producers are facing.

When viewed from this perspective, the dollar's rise since the beginning of 2015 is a natural outcome of differing policy responses in the USA versus its trading partners. In the event that the US economy were to slow in the balance of 2016, one should be wary of politicians who blame China and other countries for manipulating their exchange rates, when movements of the dollar in fact have been closely tied to changes in monetary policies at home and abroad.

Notes

1. For an excellent summary see *BCA Special Report*, "The Chinese Economy at a Critical Juncture," September 23, 2011. Readers interested in an interpretation of the various stages of China's growth should see Michael Pettis' blog *China Financial Markets*. The entry of June 18, 2014 contains an interesting discussion entitled "The four stages of Chinese growth." Another excellent source is the book by Ezra F. Vogel, *Deng Xiaoping and the Transformation of China*.
2. Data cited in this section is from *BCA Special Report*, "China: Growth Drivers and Long Term Challenges," November 4, 2009.
3. See, for example, Martin Wolf's commentary, "Why China's Economy Might Topple," *Financial Times*, April 3, 2013.
4. *BCA Special Report*, op. cit.
5. Dan Rohr, "China's Unsustainable Investment Boom," Morningstar, September 16, 2011.

6. Barclays Capital Economic Research, "China Beyond the Miracle," Part 1, September 5, 2011.
7. *Financial Times*, August 21, 2015.
8. Citi Research, "Is China Leading the World into Recession," September 8, 2015.
9. Mizuho Securities Asia Ltd., "China's 2015 Stimulus package," August 14, 2015.
10. Nomura Global Economics, Asia Special Report, "China: Rising Risks of Financial Crisis," March 15, 2013, p. 5.
11. Ibid., p. 7.
12. See Robert Z. Aliber's commentary, "One More Note on China," September 5, 2015.

12

Guidelines for Investing During Crises

In this chapter we return to a question that was raised at the outset: What guidelines should investors follow in managing portfolios during crisis situations? This issue is pertinent, because while the precepts of modern portfolio theory may apply when markets function normally, they do not hold during asset bubbles or financial crises when (private-sector) financial assets are all highly correlated. Yet little has been written to guide investors about what to do in these circumstances.

One of the central messages of this book is that investors have had to cope with a wide array of shocks from the breakdown of Bretton Woods to present, and the optimal strategies have varied considerably. While the shocks were multifaceted, they had one element in common—namely, they described situations in which markets operated in a state of disequilibrium. In some instances, the shocks were exogenous (or external) in nature—e.g., the spike in oil prices in the 1970s and early 1980s and the surge in technology stocks in the late 1990s. However, in the majority of cases the disequilibrium was partly a function of economic policies that officials were compelled to alter to restore market equilibrium.

One of the objectives of this chapter is to illustrate how the nature of the crises evolved over time as international capital mobility increased, financial systems were deregulated and financial leverage multiplied. A central issue we examine is whether there are observable patterns of behavior that investors could exploit in positioning portfolios. We begin by considering how currency crises have evolved for advanced economies that can issue debt denominated in the home currency, as well as for developing countries that must finance their imbalances by borrowing in foreign currencies. We next examine factors that have contributed to a series of asset bubbles and financial crises in

© The Editor(s) (if applicable) and The Author(s) 2016
N.P. Sargen, *Global Shocks*, DOI 10.1007/978-3-319-41105-7_12

the past 25 years, and we explain why they have posed greater challenges for investors and policymakers than traditional currency crises. Finally, we conclude by describing the unique challenge that the 2008–09 global financial crisis posed for investors, illustrating this by looking at the way in which our firm navigated through the worst crisis since the Great Depression.

The Evolving Nature of Currency Crises

Throughout this book we have distinguished between the varying challenges that currency crises and asset bubbles have posed for investors. The primary finding is that while both types of shocks required investors to adapt to surprise developments, there were systematic patterns of market movements in the currency crises, whereas the asset bubbles that ensued had a greater dispersion of outcomes due to differences in policy responses. One of the main challenges investors confronted was that the pattern of market responses to global shocks shifted over time in terms of movements of interest rates, exchange rates and asset values. Consequently, investors had to have a clear understanding of the nature of the shock, the policy response and the market response in order to cope successfully with them.

First, consider how the nature of currency crises discussed in this book changed since the breakdown of the Bretton Woods fixed exchange rate system, as illustrated in Table 12.1. During the 1970s, global investors for the most part could rely on standard economics textbooks to guide them in positioning portfolios, as the principal drivers of exchange rates were inflation rate differentials and trade and current account imbalances. The breakdown of Bretton Woods was caused by a shift in the status of the USA from being a low-inflation country to a high-inflation country as a result of expansionary monetary and fiscal policies. During this period, market participants focused on the loss of US price competitiveness as US inflation accelerated, and policymakers became concerned when the US trade and current account positions shifted from surpluses into deficits. However, the Federal Reserve was not pro-active in combatting inflation, and it was continually "behind the

Table 12.1 Evolution of currency crises, 1970s–90s

	Advanced economies	Emerging economies
1970s	Chronic dollar weakness (Fed gradualism)	"Old style" crises
1980s	Dollar overshoots (Fed regime shift)	"Old style" crises (MBAs)
1990s	Risk on/risk off (attack on ERM)	"New style" crises (Asian crisis)

curve" in raising interest rates. Thus, the terms on which the USA financed its imbalances became increasingly unfavorable, as investors required larger interest rate premiums for holding dollar-denominated assets, and it operated in the "crisis zone" for most of the decade. The winning strategy in these circumstances was to be long low-yielding currencies such as deutsche marks, Swiss francs and Japanese yen, because the depreciation of the dollar exceeded the respective interest rate differentials.

The fundamental change that occurred in the 1980s was the Federal Reserve's actions under Paul Volcker to abandon its policy of gradualism in favor of "shock therapy" in order to convince investors of its commitment to tackle inflation and to support the dollar. In this context, investors increasingly focused on the growth of money supply as the main driver of inflation and Fed policy. As US interest rates surged and interest rate differentials moved increasingly in favor of the dollar, the US currency strengthened steadily, and changes in interest rate differentials and in inflation expectations became the key drivers of exchange rates.

One of the challenges investors confronted in this period was to determine when the dollar's appreciation would elicit a change in the pro-dollar stance of the Reagan administration and also cause the Federal Reserve to ease monetary policy. My colleague, John Lipsky, and I concluded that the turning point occurred in early 1985 when the US economy showed signs of slowing materially while the US trade deficit continued to climb, as this combination of outcomes provided convincing evidence that the dollar was significantly overvalued. As the dollar declined steadily in the next two years, we subsequently questioned when officials would have to act to stabilize it, and we conceived the clockwise rotation around the quadrant diagram shown in Chapters 1 and 4, which was ultimately confirmed.

From the 1990s onward, the Fed and other major central banks were well on their way to bringing down inflation rates toward the 2 % targets they set as a goal for monetary policy. The convergence of inflation rates, in turn, meant that inflation differentials played less of a role in determining values for the US dollar and other key currencies than previously, and the period of chronic dollar crises also came to an end. Instead, a new pattern of behavior became evident during the attack on the exchange rate mechanism (ERM) in the early 1990s, when markets shifted from being in "risk on" mode, in which high-yielding currencies outperformed low-yielding ones, to being in "risk off" mode, in which the opposite pattern held. This same pattern of behavior was evident during the attack on the eurozone earlier in this decade.

Emerging Economies: Transition from "Old Style" to "New Style" Crises

Turning to emerging economies, which are depicted in the second column of Table 12.1, we distinguish between classic or "old-style" crises that prevailed in the 1970s and 1980s and "new-style" crises that became prevalent from the 1990s onward. During the 1970s and 1980s, for example, the task of identifying problem countries was straightforward. For the most part, they were ones that ran large budget and current account deficits and that were prone to high inflation. The respective central banks typically would defend the exchange rate by selling foreign exchange reserves and/or by raising interest rates, but once reserves were depleted a full-blown currency crisis ensued. Accordingly, investors would focus on the size of the budget and external payments imbalances, the growth of money supply, the rate of inflation and the level of foreign exchange reserves (in relation to imports) as key variables to identify countries whose currencies were at risk.

The less developed countries' debt crisis in the early 1980s proved to be much more extreme than previous crises, as the major debtor countries in Latin America were unable to service their debts to multinational banks and foreign governments. In this instance, commercial banks that extended loans to developing countries were able to monitor the debt with original maturities of more than one year, which was owed to foreign governments; however, there was little information on debt of less than one year's maturity or the aggregate amount that was owed to multinational banks. In these circumstances, the commercial banks responded by rolling over debt on shorter maturities (less than one year) as conditions deteriorated, but they were unaware of the extent to which others were doing the same thing. It was only after Mexico, Brazil and Argentina ran out of foreign exchange reserves that creditors understood the full magnitude of the problem.

One of the main takeaways that creditors learned from this experience was the importance of gathering timely information on the total external indebtedness of borrowing countries. Another takeaway was that it was risky to lend to governments that ran large budget deficits, because the proceeds were often wasted. The conclusion that many bankers drew was that it was preferable to lend to borrowers in the private sector, as the funds were likely to be directed to profitable investments. During the Mexican peso crisis (also known as the "Tequila crisis") of 1994–95, however, the peso sold off by about 50 % against the dollar, and the Mexican government had to be rescued by the International Monetary Fund (IMF) and the US government, when it became evident that

Mexican banks were in danger of being insolvent as a result of their borrowings in US dollars to fund investments in Mexico.

The Asian financial crisis in 1997–98 represented an even greater challenge, as the region experienced a wave of currency depreciations in countries where inflation was relatively low and public sector finances were in good shape. In this instance, the problems stemmed from a boom in commercial real estate, in which banks in the region borrowed from abroad in foreign currencies to finance loans to domestic developers. When the construction boom faded, capital flowed out of the region and Asian currencies plummeted. Central banks responded in classic fashion by tightening monetary policies, but their banking systems were threatened, because banks suffered declines in asset values while their borrowing costs increased. This situation introduced a new dimension of risk that international creditors had to consider—namely, the need to assess the health of the domestic banking systems. The "new style" of emerging market crises meant investors had to pay greater attention to analyzing balance sheet positions of borrowers and financial institutions.

Emergence of Asset Bubbles and Financial Crises

If inflation is "always and everywhere a monetary phenomenon," as Milton Friedman maintained, rapid credit expansion is the counterpart for the creation of asset bubbles. During the 1990s and ensuing period, the Federal Reserve and central banks succeeded in bringing inflation down to acceptable levels; however, they paid less attention to the growth of credit in the private sector. The ratio of US non-federal debt to gross domestic product (GDP), for example, rose from just over 1.0 times GDP in the mid-1980s to approach a peak of 2.0 times GDP on the eve of the global financial crisis.[1] The ratio for total financial assets, which includes households, corporations and financial institutions, also doubled over this period, rising from five times GDP to ten times.[2]

According to economic historian Alan M. Taylor, the explosion in private sector credit that occurred altered the financial landscape fundamentally and ushered in what he calls "The Age of Credit":

> Although broad money relative to GDP remained almost flat at around 0.7 (rising a little only in the 2000s), the asset side of banks' balance sheets exploded. Loans to GDP doubled from 0.5 to 1.0 and assets to GDP tripled from about 0.7 to roughly 2. The decoupling of loans from broad money reflected the rise of nonmonetary liabilities on bank balance sheets, such as wholesale funding. The even faster expansion of bank assets reflected this too, plus the rise in more interbank lending.[3]

The end game of all of this was a major increase in the degree of leverage in the US financial system relative to the prior trend: "In the end the banking system, insured against one type of run, can be seen to have endogenously switched over time to alternative funding sources, like wholesale, which had no such insurance, at least explicitly."[4] The bottom line is that the rapid expansion of private sector credit and the evolution of the financial system away from traditional bank lending to alternative funding sources became the source of asset bubbles that occurred in the USA, as well as other advanced economies. The 2008–09 financial crisis, in short, answered the question people had been asking for decades—namely, are there limits to how much debt the US economy can absorb without experiencing a financial crisis?

By now there is greater appreciation of the role that rapid expansion of credit has played in the creation of asset bubbles, and researchers at the Bank for International Settlements (BIS) have done an excellent job in analyzing the determinants of financial cycles. According to their research, credit aggregates, as a proxy for leverage, and property prices, as a measure of collateral, play a particularly important role in determining financial cycles, which typically last 15–20 years, and which can span several business cycles. At the same time, this poses a major challenge for investors, because the build-up of debt can last for a long time before the "Minsky moment" arrives and the bubble bursts. Also, it is more difficult to predict the way policymakers will respond to an asset bubble than to a typical currency problem. Thus, whereas the Bank of Japan and East Asian central banks tightened monetary policies when their asset bubbles burst, the Federal Reserve reduced interest rates to historic lows after both the tech bubble burst and during the global financial crisis of 2008.

The situation today is especially complex, as China and other countries in Asia have experienced a rapid build-up in debt that has been financed domestically, rather than via borrowing from abroad. With many Asian countries having acquired massive foreign exchange reserves over the past 15 years and inflation very low, they do not confront a traditional currency crisis. The debt build-up, however, has given rise to excess capacity in real estate and manufacturing that could become a full-fledged asset bubble at some point. For the time being, China's policymakers have the flexibility to postpone the day of reckoning by easing monetary policy and pursuing added fiscal stimulus, such that conditions could unfold differently than in Japan or the USA. However, to the extent that bad loans are being rolled over by government edict, a further slowing of China's economy seems inevitable. The key issue for investors in these circumstances is to ascertain whether China's slowdown will be gradual, as is currently priced into markets, or more precipitous, which is not priced into markets. At the same time, plummeting commodity prices have left commodity producers such as Brazil, Venezuela, Russia and others at risk of defaulting on their external debt.

Recognizing the evolving nature of currency crises and asset bubbles over the past 45 years or so, one may ask where this leaves us today. From my perspective, one of the most difficult challenges is to peer inside the black boxes of financial systems and identify the leverage and inter-connectedness that is embedded in them. Research by BIS on bank exposures and financial cycles is particularly useful, as it provides an analytic framework for assessing risks in financial systems, as well as monitoring the conditions in advanced and emerging economies on an ongoing basis.[5] And work now being undertaken by the Federal Reserve, US Treasury and IMF to identify macro-prudential risks should prove valuable, as well.

Still, in the end, investment professionals must make judgments when they do not have complete information. For this reason, my colleagues and I now look at a broad array of market indicators that will provide clues about possible stresses and strains in the system. We also have developed a set of indicators to monitor conditions in the credit markets because they provided early warning signals leading up to the financial crisis. Ultimately, my hope is that the economics profession will take up the challenge of understanding better the credit creation process, because it holds the key to assessing potential booms and busts in asset markets and financial systems.

Perspectives on the 2008–09 Global Financial Crisis

Of the episodes in this book, the most challenging for investors, by far, was the 2008 global financial crisis, which posed the greatest threat to the international financial system since the Great Depression. First, it began in a small segment of the financial system—subprime mortgaged-backed securities—and then spread over time to impact not only US credit markets, but those in other parts of the world as well. Like many diseases, people were not aware of the way the financial system was becoming infected, even though there were increasing symptoms of problems from the middle of 2007. By the time Lehman Brothers collapsed in September 2008 and the full extent of the problem became apparent, it was too late for policymakers to prevent a near free-fall in prices of financial assets, including highly rated corporate bonds that had been considered to be extremely safe. The broad nature of the sell-off across asset classes and around the world meant that portfolio diversification offered investors little or no protection. Since then, the question I have considered many times is "what should an investor do in these circumstances?"

One response might be that events such as the 2008 global financial crisis are extremely rare, or "black swans," and there is no basis for making broad generalizations about them. If that is true, investors should simply do their best to ride out a storm and hope another one does not come along. My own take is that this might be acceptable if asset bubbles and financial crises were rare; however, as is evident from the cases presented in this book, they in fact have become more prevalent in the past 25 years.

Furthermore, some observers may conclude that while portfolio diversification may not hold in the short run after a bubble bursts, it still is applicable for investing over the long term. I have some sympathy for this argument, as there is a tendency for people to react to a sell-off in knee-jerk fashion by unloading holdings at exactly the wrong time. But I also believe financial advisors should not oversell the benefits of international diversification: They need to acknowledge that the process of globalization, in which financial markets have become increasingly linked to one another, implies there has been a secular increase in correlations across markets. Stated simply, the benefits of diversification are not as great as they used to be before globalization became prevalent.

A natural response for investors in these circumstances might be to position portfolios defensively by paring back on risk assets and raising cash or adding to holdings of treasuries. There is certainly logic to this approach during the bust phase of a market cycle, when confusion and fear reins. But this begs the issue of when to reinvest funds. This decision is critical for capitalizing on markets that are oversold. However, it is not easy to implement, because the natural inclination for people is to be gun-shy following a market collapse.

For this reason, it is important to formulate a strategy that will protect portfolios during the down phase of a cycle, while also being prepared to take advantage of oversold conditions in markets. I maintain that the critical factor in deciding when to redeploy assets is having confidence that policies are in place to stabilize the situation. This approach is illustrated in the way our parent firm, Western & Southern, navigated the global financial crisis. While our investment team encountered numerous challenges during the 2008 sell-off phase, the plan for reinvesting funds was implemented in stages beginning in late 2008, and it enabled our firm to benefit from the huge rally over the next five years.

Guiding Principle: The Importance of a Value Discipline

The guiding principle of Fort Washington Investment Advisors, which is the investment affiliate of the Western & Southern Financial Group, is to out-perform markets over the long term while pursuing a rigorous value disci-pline. One of the virtues of this approach is that portfolio managers who are value-oriented are less likely to be victims of irrational exuberance than momentum-based investors or closet indexers who are trend followers. At the same time, we recognize that having a value discipline does not mean one will always outperform the markets. In fact, the most challenging times for value managers occur when markets are frenzied and ignore valuations. It would be easier to deal with these situations if they did not last very long. However, the experiences of the past two decades suggest otherwise.

When markets form bubbles and valuations are stretched, investors face two sets of challenges. One is to outlast the market overshoot, and the other is to diagnose the problem correctly. The Harvard Business School case study about Grantham, Mayo and van Otterloo in Chapter 9 describes how dif-ficult this was during the tech boom, when it lost half of its assets under management.

While Jeremy Grantham is critical of portfolio managers who are closet indexers, my own perspective is that it is okay to hide behind a benchmark temporarily if you are confused or unsure as to what is happening. I learned this lesson initially in the late 1990s when I misdiagnosed the situation in Southeast Asia, and also when I was premature in calling an end to the bull market in tech stocks. Both of these experiences helped prepare me for what turned out to be the greatest challenge of my career in navigating through the turmoil surrounding the global financial crisis.

The Importance of Staying Flexible

One of the main lessons I learned throughout my career is the importance of staying flexible when a crisis situation is developing, because the initial diag-nosis of a problem may be wrong. This lesson was particularly applicable in 2007, when I began to focus on problems in the subprime sector of the US housing market. My initial inclination was that this segment was too small to undermine the US economy, and I took comfort when officials at the Federal Reserve downplayed its significance.

My perception of the situation changed in August, however, when the European Central Bank and the Federal Reserve were required to provide liquidity to commercial banks in response to a seizing up of credit markets in Europe. This development was accompanied by a widening in credit spreads for the first time since 2002, and our fixed-income portfolio managers became concerned about diminished liquidity in the US bond market. I became worried that a tightening of credit market conditions could have a more significant impact on the economy than I previously expected.

When the US stock market began to sell off in the fourth quarter, my colleague John O'Connor and I agreed it was time to develop a plan to pare back equity positions for our parent, especially in US financials, where the firm had a large overweight position. Our idea was to build a "war chest" that would enable us to buy back assets cheaper once the market shakeout was over. The plan was approved by our Risk Management Committee, and we began to implement it soon after. However, we paused in selling bank stocks after the collapse of Bear Sterns in March, when the stock market rallied as the Fed lowered the funds rate from 3 % to 2 %.

Meanwhile, circumstances caused us to shift attention back to the US bond market, as credit spreads continued to widen and the market for non-agency mortgage-backed securities ground to a halt. Our investment professionals discovered how illiquid the credit markets had become when they attempted to exit certain positions, and we were surprised by how far the prices for highly rated bonds had fallen. The situation continued to deteriorate throughout the summer, as problems spread to the federally sponsored mortgage institutions and to major financial institutions.

When Lehman Brothers folded in mid-September, panic set in and money-market funds became threatened. We discovered there were few places to hide other than cash, gold and US treasuries when markets collapsed. One of the biggest surprises was to see the value of our corporate bonds plummet well below their par values, as yields for investment-grade bonds approached 10 % on average and those for high-yield bonds were in the vicinity of 20 %. The lack of liquidity in fixed income markets made it expensive to liquidate assets and, in the case of structured products, markets ceased to function.

Therefore, during the panic phase that ensued after the collapse of Lehman Brothers, we had little choice but to hold on to bond positions and ride out the storm, while paring back on equities as needed. While we were shocked by what ensued, we nonetheless took comfort that our investment portfolios were well diversified and our bond portfolios were high quality overall. Therefore, we expected them to rebound once financial conditions stabilized.

Capitalizing on Oversold Markets

As risk assets plummeted in value in the fourth quarter of 2008, we became more convinced they were oversold, but we were uncertain when to begin redeploying funds into the markets. We understood that the best time to act is when sentiment has turned overwhelmingly bearish and people are scared. Jeremy Grantham summed it up very well in an article titled "Reinvesting When Terrified" when he wrote:

> There is only one cure for terminal paralysis: you must have a battle plan for reinvestment and stick to it. Since every action must overcome paralysis what I recommend is a few large steps, not many small ones… *Remember that you will never catch the low.*[6]

In our case, we made the decision to reinvest funds in stages, beginning in late 2008. We recognized how precarious the situation was for the economy and financial institutions, but we drew comfort that policymakers acknowledged the systemic problems and the Federal Reserve acted decisively in easing monetary policy.

In light of the tremendous uncertainty at the time, we decided the best strategy was to proceed in stages. The initial foray was to add to holdings of investment-grade corporate bonds in December, when the head of fixed income, Roger Lanham, became convinced that the surge in corporate bond yields was the best buying opportunity in his career. Soon after, we added to exposure in BB- and B-rated high-yield bonds, as our lead portfolio manager, Brendan White, maintained we were well compensated for credit risks. His call proved prescient, as only one bond in the portfolio eventually defaulted, and high yield proved to be the best-performing asset class for several years.

The decision to reinvest in equities was influenced by Jamie Wilhelm, who was responsible for our Focused Equity portfolio and is a keen student of market history. Jamie first urged me to add to equity positions in late 2008, when the S&P 500 index had fallen to a level of 750, which he calculated to be equivalent to the market trading at its replacement cost. However, I held off implementing his recommendation, because I was not sure whether the banking system was stable at that time.

I became more confident about the stability of the financial system during early 2009, when the Troubled Asset Relief Program (TARP) proceeds were converted to a program designed to recapitalize troubled banks. Soon after, the majority of financial institutions passed the stress tests that were conducted to determine whether they had adequate capital, and we began to add to equity holdings. Even though many investors at the time maintained that the subsequent run-up in the stock market was entirely the result of the Fed's accommodative stance, we disagreed. Our view was that equity market valuations were reasonable at the time and the outlook for corporate profits was favorable, because US companies were able to adapt to an environment of moderate economic growth.

In looking back at our ability to survive the turmoil and ultimately to benefit from the market rebound that ensued, I have greater appreciation for the strength of our firm's balance sheet. John Barrett, the head of our firm, has been a long-time champion of maintaining a capital-asset ratio that is among the highest in the financial services industry. And while the ratio fell to a low of 10 % during the worst stretch of the financial crisis, it was still considerably above ratios maintained by most financial institutions, and it currently is at 18 %. As a result, our firm never confronted a situation in which we were forced out of positions by adverse market developments, and we had the luxury of knowing we were well-capitalized to ride out the storm.

The story had a happy ending both for our parent and for outside clients: Western & Southern's balance sheet today is the strongest in its 126-year history, and since the end of 2008 the investment results for outside clients have been the best in its 25-year history of Fort Washington Investment Advisors, due in part to efforts to improve our investment processes and risk-control procedures.

Conclusions

There are several takeaways from this case study:

- First, managing money during asset bubbles and financial crises is one of the most challenging experiences for any investor, and it is inherently difficult to time them. Because the circumstances are often complex and very fluid, your initial assessment may be incorrect. Therefore, one needs to stay flexible, and the primary objective should be to ensure you can survive a major market sell-off.
- The best way to guard against irrational behavior is to have a value orientation. When asset values become stretched, it is prudent to pare back holdings and raise cash and/or reduce overweight positions in risk assets, especially when there are signs of credit problems or inflation. However, one must also be prepared for asset values to stay stretched for long periods.

- An investor should have a plan in place for redeploying assets when they are oversold, as this is the best opportunity to outperform the market substantially. I favor doing so in stages, rather than all at once or in small incremental moves.
- A financial institution that has a strong balance sheet has an advantage over ones that do not, in that it has the wherewithal to ride out the storm and is less prone to be forced out of positions.

Finally, these precepts served our firm very well during the global financial crisis, and I believe they are applicable to future crises as well.

Notes

1. See BCA Special Report, "The Financial Crisis of 2007–09: Lessons learned and Where We Go From Here," June 11, 2010, p. 3.
2. Ibid., p. 4.
3. Alan M. Taylor, "The Great Leveraging" presented at the BIS Annual Conference, Lucerne, June 2012.
4. Ibid.
5. BIS 84th *Annual Report,* Chapter IV, "Debt and the financial cycle: domestic and global," June 29, 2014.
6. See GMO's website for March 2009.

About the Author

Nicholas Sargen is an international economist turned global money manager. He has been involved in international financial markets since the early 1970s, when he began his career at the US Treasury and the Federal Reserve. He subsequently worked on Wall Street for 25 years, holding senior positions with Morgan Guaranty Trust, Salomon Brothers Inc., Prudential Insurance and J.P. Morgan Private Bank. In 2003 he became Chief Investment Officer for the Western & Southern Financial Group and its affiliate, Fort Washington Investment Advisors Inc., where he now serves as Chief Economist.

Sargen has written extensively on international financial markets, and he currently produces a blog, *Fort Washington Focus*, on his website, where his views are updated. He appeared frequently on business television programs throughout his career on Wall Street and was a regular panelist on Louis Rukeyser's *Wall Street Week*.

Sargen was born and raised in the San Francisco Bay Area, and received a Ph.D. in Economics from Stanford University. He is also an adjunct professor at the University of Virginia's Darden School of Business.

© The Editor(s) (if applicable) and The Author(s) 2016
N.P. Sargen, *Global Shocks*, DOI 10.1007/978-3-319-41105-7

Index

Note: Page numbers with "n" denote notes.

© The Editor(s) (if applicable) and The Author(s) 2016
N.P. Sargen, *Global Shocks*, DOI 10.1007/978-3-319-41105-7

Printed in the United States of America